WHAT CATS WANT

BLOOMSBURY PUBLISHING
Bloomsbury Publishing Plc
50 Bedford Square, London, WC1B 3DP, UK

BLOOMSBURY, BLOOMSBURY PUBLISHING and the
Diana logo are trademarks of Bloomsbury Publishing Plc

Originally published in Japanese by X-Knowledge Co., Ltd., Tokyo

This English language edition published by arrangement with
X-Knowledge Co., Ltd., Tokyo c/o Tuttle-Mori Agency, Inc., Tokyo

First published in Great Britain 2020

English language translation by George Miller, 2020

A catalogue record for this book is available from the British Library

Library of Congress Cataloguing-in-Publication data has been applied for

ISBN: HB: 978-1-5266-2306-5, eBook: 978-1-5266-2307-2

6 8 10 9 7 5

The publishers would like to thank Jo Ireson for her guidance on feline care for the English language edition of this book

Book design by Guillaume Arduré

Typesetting by Thomas Bohm, User Design, Illustration and Typesetting, UK

Printed and bound in Italy by Printer Trento Srl

WHAT CATS WANT

An illustrated guide for *truly* understanding your cat

DR. YUKI HATTORI

BLOOMSBURY PUBLISHING
LONDON • OXFORD • NEW YORK • NEW DELHI • SYDNEY

ABOUT THIS BOOK

Every cat owner wants to enjoy the time they spend with their pet and look after them well. This book contains tips to help you do just that.

Cats have an air of mystery and can sometimes seem aloof and unpredictable. This reputation probably stems from the fact that they live life at their own rhythm and can be stubborn. But in reality, cats are highly sensitive creatures who express a multitude of feelings through their body language. When you know how to read them, you'll discover that every expression, however insignificant, has a meaning. You'll never look at your cat in the same way again!

Domestic cats' life expectancy has been steadily rising, and it's not uncommon now to come across cats aged over twenty. To give your cat a long and healthy life, you need to provide her with a good diet and pay attention to her health so that you quickly spot anything untoward. Her longevity depends on the love and attention you give her. To live happily with your cat, you need to really get to know her. This book will give you advice on understanding you cat's behaviour, providing her with the best environment and maintaining her health. And, of course, that simple tip applies to all cats, male as well as female!

I would be delighted if this book could be of some use to cats and their owners.

CONTENTS

CHAPTER 2:
DETECTIVE WORK

CHAPTER 3:
EVERYDAY CARE

CHAPTER 4:
MAKING YOUR CAT HAPPY

CHAPTER 5:

CREATING A CAT-FRIENDLY HOME

Extra notes

CHAPTER 6:

A LONG AND HAPPY LIFE

TEN BASIC RULES FOR UNDERSTANDING CATS

1 **Take the time to learn the secrets of a cat's life.**

My hearing is so sharp that I can hear an ant's footsteps (page 18). I always land on my paws (page 73). But don't forget that I also have weak points! (Pages 14–26.)

2 **Try to understand your cat's state of mind.**

By paying attention to my miaows and body language, you'll find it easy to understand my feelings and emotions (pages 40–82).

3 **Remember that some of the foods and smells that humans enjoy are harmful for cats.**

There are some common plants and essential oils which could even kill me (pages 23 and 126).

4 **Keep a watchful eye on your cat, so you can detect the slightest change in behaviour.**

If I start licking myself in a way you haven't seen before or seem troubled by my joints, I may be unwell (pages 25 and 49). Take me to the vet if I'm acting strangely!

5 **Never be angry if your cat wants to mark territory in your home.**

Urine-marking and scratching are normal cat behaviours. But you can reduce or even eliminate them by having me neutered – if I'm a male cat – and giving me a scratching post (pages 66–7, 98–9 and 136–7).

6 **Provide a high-up perch or a little hidden corner for your cat.**

When I'm high up or squeezed into a narrow space, I feel completely secure. I love that! (Pages 72 and 74–5.)

7 **Be mindful of the dangers your cat may face if you let her out.**

I like looking out the window, but I don't necessarily want to go outside (pages 86–7). As an indoor cat, I'm likely to live three years longer than cats who are allowed out (page 146).

8 **To help avoid injuries or illness, take care of your cat's hygiene.**

Don't forget to brush me (pages 90–91), clean my teeth (pages 92–3) and get my claws clipped (pages 94–5) as often as necessary to avoid injuries and ailments.

9 **Play with your cat to her heart's content.**

If I'm an indoor cat, I might not get enough exercise. Try to find time to play with me every day (pages 110–11).

10 **If possible, put some money aside to care for me.**

It's likely you'll need to spend a lot of money on me over the years, so can you start saving a bit to cover the cost? You should also consider pet insurance (pages 150–51).

CHAPTER 1 THE BODY AND ITS MYSTERIES

CAT BIOLOGY

SECRETS IN THEIR EYES

A cat's eyes shine in the dark because of a reflective layer behind the retina which is called the *tapetum lucidum* (bright tapestry). This layer, which humans lack, makes cats' eyes 40% more effective than ours at capturing light.

SO-SO SIGHT

Although cats are very good at detecting moving objects, their eyesight is poor, between 2/10 and 3/10. In the past, spotting prey in motion would have been more important for their hunting ancestors than being able to see an inanimate object.

Cats' eyes are perfectly adapted for night vision though: their pupils can dilate to three times the size of ours and capture six times more light. This enables them to be active at dawn and dusk and explains their reputation as nocturnal creatures. Cats also have a wider field of view than us.

1

Stationary objects are invisible

Because of their poor eyesight, cats may not see static objects, but they compensate for this with a wide field of view, high sensitivity to light and an acute sense of hearing.

Cats can't see red
It's also believed that black looks the same as red to cats, but they can tell the difference between yellow and blue.

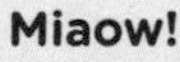

Mirrors of the soul
A cat's eyes – like her whiskers and ears – look different depending on how she feels (see pages 27 and 65).

2

Pupils that shrink and dilate

If it's bright, a cat's pupils will shrink to protect the retina of her eyes. In lower light, her pupils will dilate to let in more light. They will also dilate when she is excited or anxious.

3

All kittens have blue eyes

It's only around the age of three months that the pigments in a cat's eyes begin to work, giving them blue and green tints. Because of a genetic quirk, Siamese and Himalayan cats will keep their blue eyes into adulthood.

Colourpoint cats
Siamese and Himalayan cats are known as "colourpoints". As well as blue eyes, these breeds have pale bodies and darker-coloured extremities: ears, muzzle, paws and tail. The extremities are the least warm parts of the body.

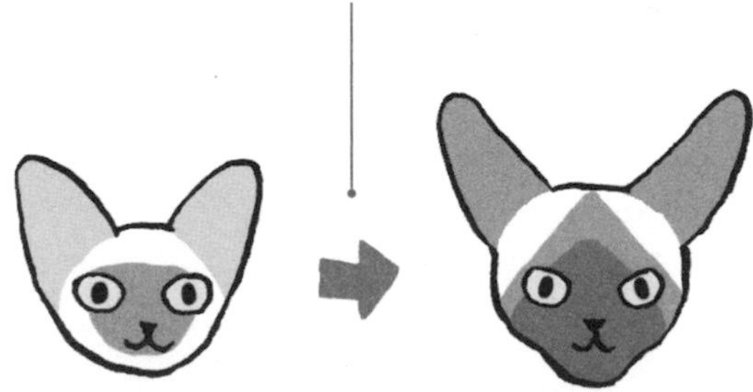

CAT BIOLOGY

YOU CAN TELL A LOT FROM A CAT'S EYES

Your cat's eyes can often alert you to any general health problems that she may develop. Note the condition of her eyes and regularity of her blinking every day.

EYES THAT CAN'T OPEN OR CLOSE ARE A BAD SIGN

Cats' corneas are not very sensitive, so a speck of dust in their eyes doesn't generally bother them and they shouldn't need to blink very often.

That means frequent blinking is a cause for concern, as are droopy eyelids, which stop the eyes from opening properly.

And if you notice anything unusual about your cat's tear ducts or an increased amount of sleep or tears in their eyes, you should consult your vet at once.

1

Gunky eyes or tears

White or greenish-yellow secretion in a cat's eyes may be a sign of a bacterial infection. Persistently weepy eyes can be caused by a damaged cornea. In both cases, your cat will need to see a vet. (Flat-faced breeds, such as Persians, have persistently weepy eyes anyway, because of the narrowness of their tear ducts. Their eyes need frequent wiping.)

Something's wrong!
Rub! Rub!

Stop scratching
There are times when your cat may need a cone-shaped recovery collar to stop her from rubbing her eyes.

Don't hurt me!

2

Yellowish whites

The yellowing of the whites of a cat's eyes may be a sign of jaundice or liver problems. But as this part of a cat's eyes is rarely visible, you should get into the habit of raising her eyelids from time to time to check.

Check the whites of her eyes
If signs of jaundice are already visible, it's time for a trip to the vet.

3

The "nictitating membrane"

The membrane at the inner corner of the eye is also sometimes called the "third eyelid". Its role is to cover and protect a cat's eyes when they're closed. If you can see this membrane when your cat's eyes are open, she may be unwell.

Look me in the eye!
Nictitating membrane

Not to be confused
Don't mix up the iris (the coloured part around the pupil) and the "white" of the eye.

Pupil size
If your cat has one pupil bigger than the other, this may indicate a health problem.

CAT BIOLOGY

LISTENING CAREFULLY

Hearing is a cat's most highly developed sense, and one which is very handy for stalking prey in low light.

HEARING IS A CAT'S STRONGEST SENSE

Your cat's hearing is more sensitive than ours or a dog's, which enables her to hunt at night and even detect the sound of an ant in the grass.

Their hearing is especially acute at high frequencies. This is partly because of the high-pitched sounds of the favourite prey: mice.

If your cat doesn't respond when you call her, don't worry, it doesn't mean she has a hearing problem. Although it's true that older cats can become hard of hearing...

1

A winning trio: hearing, smell and sight

Cats' sharpest senses, in descending order, are hearing, smell and sight. They have evolved to be skilled nocturnal hunters.

Waiting patiently
Have you found your cat waiting at the door when you come home? She has recognized the sound of your footsteps or your car.

2

Cats don't hear bass notes

A cat's hearing range is between 40 Hz and 65,000 Hz, whereas ours is 20 Hz to 20,000 Hz. This means that they are very good at detecting high-pitched sounds, but less good at hearing lower sounds.

Cats like women's voices
The human voice is generally pitched in the range 200 Hz to 2,000 Hz. Cats seem more drawn to women's voices than men's, probably because of their preference for higher frequencies.

3

Cats hear things we can't

If your cat appears to be staring into space, she's probably listening to something you can't hear, such as an insect's wings beating or the sound of small rodents.

Hearing loss with age
Cats often ignore their owners' call simply because they're not interested. But sometimes this is because of hearing loss due to age or illness. It's hard to measure a cat's hearing accurately, but if she doesn't react to loud noises such as thunder, she's likely to be hard of hearing.

CAT BIOLOGY

A GOOD SENSE OF SMELL

A cat might use her sense of smell to locate anything from prey to potential rivals, or even just her food bowl. If you warm her food, you'll help stimulate her appetite by enhancing its smell.

BETTER AT SMELLING THAN HUMANS, BUT LESS GOOD THAN DOGS

Cats have 65 million olfactory receptors (compared to just ten million in humans). A German shepherd, meanwhile, has around 200 million, which explains its popularity as a police dog.

Flat-faced cats have a less developed sense of smell than those with longer faces because of their narrower nasal cavity. A cat's sense of smell helps her identify prey and predators, and also helps her decide whether a bit of food is safe to eat. All these faculties are vital for a solitary animal such as the cat.

1
Nose-rubbing

It's not uncommon to see two cats greet each other by touching noses. Sometimes cats will also touch their nose to their owner's hand, likewise a sign of greeting. She's more likely to do this if you proffer a finger rather than your whole hand, which may scare her.

A sign of affection
Touching noses is a sign of affection between cats. If your cat touches you with her nose, then you've won her trust.

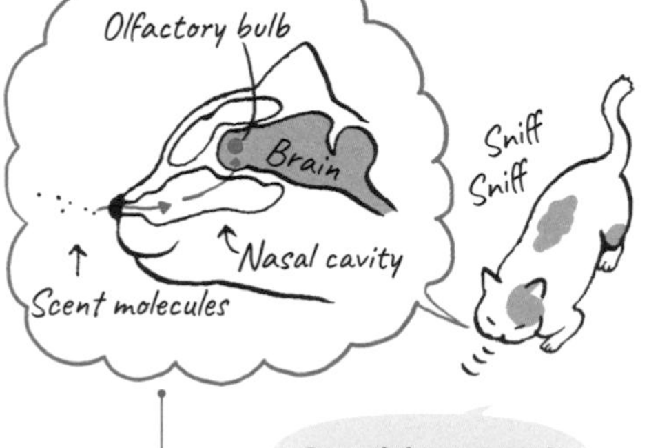

2
A cat's nasal cavity

When scent molecules enter your cat's nose, they're detected by her olfactory cells, then turned into nerve impulses and sent to her brain. That's where she stores her library of smells, including the smell of you!

Sensitive nose!

Nose hairs
Unlike us, cats have no nose hairs. The reason for this isn't known. Nose hairs are certainly useful for stopping dust from entering our nasal cavity.

3
Scent preferences

Many cats like the minty smell of cat-friendly toothpaste. Few of them are fond of the smell of citrus. But there are always exceptions...

Yuck!

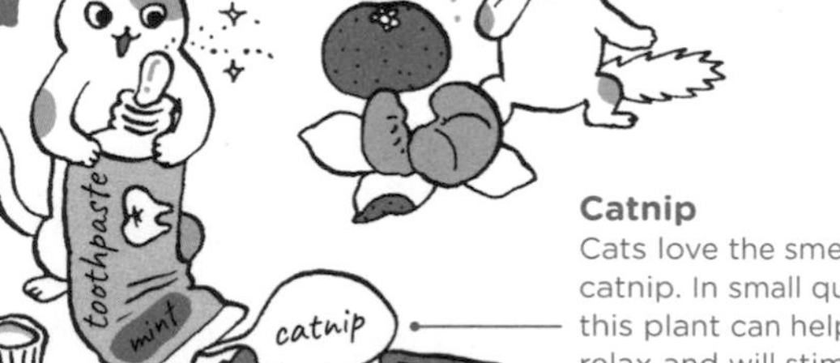

Catnip
Cats love the smell of catnip. In small quantities, this plant can help them relax and will stimulate their appetite.

CAT BIOLOGY

IS A WET NOSE GOOD?

Generally, a wet nose is a good sign, but if your cat's nose is constantly runny, it's time for a trip to the vet.

RUNNY NOSE AND SNEEZES

A healthy cat's nose will be slightly damp. This means she can capture a maximum number of smells, since scent molecules are more easily picked up by a damp nose.

This dampness is maintained by the imperceptible secretion of nasal fluid and saliva through capillary action. But if a runny nose becomes more persistent, it may be because of a viral infection of the upper respiratory tract. If your cat has a nosebleed, she may have a tumour. In both cases, she needs to go to the vet. Don't forget to give your vet useful information such as the quantity, colour and consistency of the nasal fluid or blood, when the symptoms began and whether it is affecting both nostrils or just one side.

1

What about a dry nose?

When your cat's awake, her nose should be slightly damp. If it isn't, she's probably dehydrated. To encourage her to drink, try changing the temperature of her water slightly, or see pages 32–3 for more ideas.

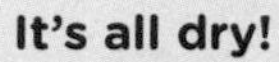

It's all dry!

Dry air and smell
If your cat's nose is dry, it may be because the ambient air is dry too. This can cause olfactory mucus to dry out, followed by an immune deficiency and a cold. Sometimes, using a humidifier may be advisable.

The dangers of essential oils
It takes a lot of plant matter to make essential oils. So if your cat swallows just 1ml of essential oil, it's equivalent to ingesting several kilos of plants, which could prove fatal.

Lavender
Put that away!

2

Essential oils are out

Using an essential oil diffuser is not recommended if you have a cat. She will want to get rid of the scent molecules and may ingest them by licking her coat. This could be fatal, as cats have difficulty digesting plant-based matter.

3

No smoking!

A cat who lives with a smoker has three times more risk of developing a lymphoma (malignant tumour of the lymphatic system) than one in a non-smoking household. As well as the dangers of passive smoking, a cat can ingest toxic substances deposited on her fur when grooming. For the same reason, it's best not to burn incense in a room frequented by your cat.

Outside!

Lymphoma
Lymphoma is a frequent illness for cats and has been shown to be more common if the owner smokes.

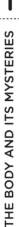

CAT BIOLOGY

MULTI-PURPOSE TONGUE

A cat uses her tongue to taste her food, lap water, groom herself and express her affection for you. But licking can also be a sign of discomfort or illness.

LICKS OF LOVE

Cats lick each other as a sign of friendship. They lick each other's faces as that's the only part of their bodies they're unable to reach with their own tongues. If your cat gives you little licks on the face or hands, she's expressing affection. But if she licks a part of her own body too insistently, it may be a sign it hurts or itches, so it's worth examining her.

She also uses her tongue to perceive taste. Cats are very sensitive to bitterness, which enables them to avoid toxic foods, which are often bitter. They can also detect umami, the so-called "fifth flavour" but they have more trouble perceiving sweet and salty flavours.

1

A comb and a file

The surface of a cat's tongue, which is covered in tiny spines, is as rough as sandpaper. A cat uses it as a comb when grooming herself.

Tongue in close-up
When your cat licks your hand, it feels like sandpaper. This roughness is due to curved, flexible spines called papillae.

Useful for lapping

Cats drink by flicking their tongue in the shape of an inverted "J" over the surface of water and then quickly retracting it. This produces a column of water that flows into their mouth thanks to a law of physics called the "inertia principle".

2

Drinking styles
The tongue takes the shape of an inverted "J" to drink from a bowl, but some cats prefer to drink from a running tap or water fountain.

3

Watch out for...
Redness or eczema in places where she licks herself and any changes in her behaviour. Such information can be useful to your vet.

Don't ignore compulsive licking

If your cat keeps licking herself in the same place, part her fur to check if she has a splinter. The problem could also be dermatological or psychological, or kitty may have fleas. If the behaviour continues, take her to the vet.

CAT BIOLOGY

WHISKERS ARE PRACTICAL AS WELL AS IMPRESSIVE

A cat's whiskers - or vibrissae, to give them their scientific name - are sense organs in their own right. When kittens are born, they use them to find their mother's teats so they can feed.

MANY WHISKERS

Cats use their vibrissae (whiskers) for feeling things and touch is just as important as hearing for them, as these senses allow them to be active at night. Whiskers are also useful for figuring out whether there's enough room to slip through a narrow passage.

Cats not only have vibrissae above their eyelids and on either side of their nose, but also on the back of their fore-legs. These hairs are longer and stiffer than the others and can detect the tiniest of vibrations through a dense network of nerve endings at their base.

1

Mood indicators

A cat expresses her mood in the way she moves her whiskers (as well as her ears and tail - see pages 44–5 and 56–7). When she's feeling inquisitive, the whiskers will be forward. But if she's afraid, she'll pull them together and draw them back against her face. If she wants to know whether she'll fit through an opening, she feels out the space with her whiskers first.

A cat's mood
When your cat's annoyed, her whiskers will fan out and point forward. But if she's calm or happy, her whiskers will look relaxed.

2

New whiskers for old

Whiskers are shed and regrow regularly, but the speed at which this happens depends on the individual.

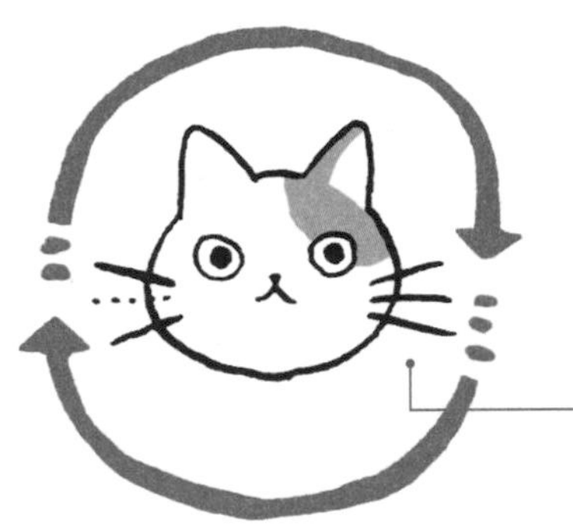

Quintessence of cat
To call something "the cat's whiskers" means it's the best of the best. Perhaps that's why cats are so proud of them.

Hair's breadth
Whiskers are around 0.3mm in diameter, which is three to six times thicker than other hairs.

Precious whiskers
The roots of a cat's whiskers are three times deeper than other hairs, so they are an important sensor.

Don't hurt me!

3

Never pull out their whiskers

As with other hair, a cat feels nothing when their whiskers fall out naturally. But if you pull them out, it will really hurt.

GOOD FOOD FOR GOOD HEALTH

It's important to give your cat a balanced diet in the right portion sizes.

THE RIGHT AMOUNT

Some cats like to empty their bowl all at once, whereas others prefer to snack throughout the day. The key thing is that she has a regular daily ration. You don't need to refill her bowl just because it's empty.

There's a risk of giving her too much food, which can lead to obesity, a condition that affects cats as well as people.

If you dispense dry food from a puzzle feeder or hide it round the house, that will encourage healthy grazing, rather than gobbling it down in one go! Wet food can be put down twice a day.

1

Eating and drinking

It's important for kitty to stay hydrated. Give her plenty of fresh water alongside her food.

Good hydration
Wet food contains 70–80% water, compared to just 5–10% in dry food.

2

A good mix

Your cat will benefit from eating a mixture of wet and dry food.

Choose the complete option
There are two sorts of cat food: "complete", which caters for all a cat's nutrition requirements, and "complimentary", which has more of some nutrients than others.

3

Food for every life stage

Kittens, adults and older cats have different nutritional needs, so choose food designed for them. The packet will tell you how much they need.

Distinct nutritional needs
At each stage of life, a cat has specific nutritional needs, so adapt her diet accordingly (see pages 158–9).

A PLEASANT DINING EXPERIENCE

Deciding where to feed your cat means taking account of cat behaviour.

NEVER NEAR THE LITTER TRAY

Cats like cleanliness. That's why their bowls should never be by their litter tray. They generally prefer their feeding and drinking bowls not to be near each other.

Even though we know what flavours cats can taste (page 24), we know little about their taste preferences and how these change with age.

1

Calculate portion size carefully

You'll always find the recommended daily portion size (determined according to the cat's weight) on the back of the packet. All you need to do is measure the right quantity for her size.

A cat's energy requirements
This depends on the weight, age and body mass of the cat. This is a complex calculation, which is why it's worth referring to the food manufacturer's guidelines.

2

Food and activity level

Your cat's daily food intake also needs to take account of whether she's active or sedentary. A less active cat should eat less food to avoid weight gain. The same goes for neutered cats.

Weight gain
If your cat has a tendency to put on weight, try cutting her daily portion size by 10–20% compared to the recommended quantity.

3

Premium food, please

Premium cat food undergoes stricter quality controls, uses better quality ingredients and provides a more balanced diet than regular food. All this comes at a price, but if you can afford it, give your cat high-quality food.

Loss of appetite
If your cat refuses her usual food for several days, take her to the vet. Cats have a sensitive palate and she may simply have detected a subtle change in the additives used, or even a change in where they were manufactured. It has been known!

WELLBEING

WATER IS VITAL

To encourage your cat to drink, always have fresh water available and know her preferences.

TAP WATER OR MINERAL WATER?

Being well hydrated is as important as good food to staying healthy. To get a better sense of your cat's preferences, try cold water, room-temperature water, filtered water and running water from the tap.

1

A clean, shallow bowl

Cats like fresh water. When the level in her bowl goes down, don't just top up what's already there. Wash the bowl, then refill it so that it's always clean. Select a shallow bowl as some cats don't like their whiskers touching the sides as they drink. They also tend to prefer ceramic or glass to plastic.

Always put the bowl far away from the litter tray
Because of their highly developed sense of smell, cats can get stressed if the place where they drink is too close to their litter tray. They may even refuse to drink.

This one's mine!

Water's not for sharing
Cats don't like sharing their water with other cats – or with dogs.

2

Multiple watering holes

Cats like to be able to drink in several different places, so it's best to have water bowls all around the house. If you have several cats, you'll need at least one bowl per cat.

3

Drinking too much or too little

If your cat's drinking more than 50ml per kilo of her body weight in twenty-four hours, it could be a sign that she's sick. Drinking too little is another possible warning sign, as it can lead to cystitis or kidney stones. The important thing is to be aware of how much your cat normally drinks so that you don't miss signs of potential health problems.

Problems specific to older cats
If an older cat starts drinking a lot of water, she may be suffering from kidney disease, an overactive thyroid or diabetes (see pages 154–5).

A CLEAN, QUIET PLACE TO GO

If your cat visits her litter tray regularly, it's a sign that she's happy with it. Don't forget to check the state of what she deposits there, as this will give you an indication of her general health.

WATCH BUT DON'T DISTURB

When all is well, a cat digs a little hole in her litter tray before urinating or defecating, then buries the result when she's finished. But if she's not happy with the tray or its position, she may stop using it.

It's important to know the normal colour, consistency, shape and smell of her poo as well as how often she goes. That way, you'll soon spot anything amiss and can quickly get her to the vet.

1

Signs of dissatisfaction

If your cat stops burying her excrement and urine, or only part-buries it, or scratches somewhere other than in her litter tray, she may be unhappy with her toilet facilities.

Scratching the wall after doing her business

It may seem as though she's just cleaning her paws, but in fact this action is a sign she's unhappy with her litter tray. Try changing the tray size, or the type and quantity of litter.

2

Litter tray cleanliness

Cats like cleanliness and have an acute sense of smell. If her toilet area is dirty, she'll refuse to use it, so urine and excrement need to be removed several times a day.

A regular wash-down

Every two to four weeks, throw out all of the used litter and replace it. Take this opportunity to thoroughly clean the tray, but avoid using detergents. It's also better not to use litter tray liners, especially scented ones.

3

Warning signs

Normally, her poo should be quite firm and the colour of milk chocolate, and deposited once or twice a day. If it's too soft or she's constipated for three days, you should take her to the vet. The same applies if you see blood in her urine or it is orange in colour.

A COSY PLACE TO SLEEP

Cats like sleeping in a high, narrow place. If you notice a change in how long your cat is sleeping, keep a close eye on her.

SIXTEEN TO SEVENTEEN HOURS' SHUT-EYE A DAY

Compared to humans, cats are big sleepers. In fact, apart from hunting, their wild ancestors spent most of their time asleep to save energy, and this habit has continued with domestic cats.

Instinctively, your cat will choose a comfy place high up to protect herself from possible predators. The ideal would be to provide several different sleeping places so that she can vary where she sleeps depending on the weather or time of year.

1
Nightly crazy half hour

In the wild, cats hunt at dusk to avoid being spotted by their prey. If your cat gets animated when you turn out the light, it's because the time for her to hunt has come.

And we're off...
What energy!

Hunting practice
If your cat rushes around in all directions, it's because she's training for hunting. If you have two cats, it's likely they will play games of cat and mouse, swapping roles from time to time.

Let me out!

2
Air-conditioning

In summer, most cats dislike being in direct contact with air from an air conditioner. If your cat sleeps in a room with air-conditioning, it's best to leave the door open so that she can come and go freely.

Change of location
Indoor cats don't sleep all day in the same place. They go from room to room for a change of sleeping position.

3
Snoring and tumour risk

There's nothing unusual about a cat snoring. But if the snoring becomes especially loud, it may be a sign of a malignant tumour in her nose.

Sleeping position
There are no inherently dangerous sleeping positions, but if your cat is sleeping in an unusual position, it may indicate joint pain. If this persists, seek veterinary advice.

EXTRA NOTES

1

A CAT FOR EVERYONE

First decide on the sex and breed of the cat you want. To do this, you need to take into account the character (see page 109) and possible health problems (pages 152–3) associated with each breed. This choice is important for finding *the* ideal cat for your household.

In a rescue centre or animal charity, you'll find a large selection to choose from: kittens, adults, pure breeds and mixed breeds. Some will already have had a medical check-up and you'll know if they have any health problems. Others may come with less information about their health.

Breeders specialize in specific breeds. If you know exactly what breed you want, you could go to a breeder.

There are a thousand and one ways to meet the cat who's right for you. But don't forget that her health and character will inevitably depend on how you look after her. Good food and an environment adapted to her needs are the key to a long, happy relationship.

CHAPTER

2

DETECTIVE WORK

INTERPRETING THEIR MIAOWS

A cat can make about twenty different noises. Let's try to interpret them.

MIAOWS IN CONTEXT

Kittens miaow to let their mother know where they are or to call for her help. Feral cats miaow to warn their rivals or signal when they're in heat. Domestic cats mainly miaow to express how they're feeling.

To understand what mood your cat's in, you need to take account not only of her miaows, but also her facial expressions and body language (see pages 44–7). You may be surprised by just how demonstrative your cat can be.

Cat Noises

Frequency	Sound	Translation	Meaning
Very often	Miaow	"I want to play!"	This is the sound cats make most often. They do it to encourage their owners to play with them, cuddle or feed them. It can also express frustration.
	Purr	"I feel happy."	A purr is the ultimate expression of wellbeing. As kittens purr almost from birth, it's likely that this sound is fundamental to communication between a mother cat and her litter. But the exact mechanism of this sound, which comes from the base of the throat, is still only partly understood. (Purrs can sometimes also mean different things, see pages 50-51.)
Occasional	Chirrup	"Hello!"	A cat uses this short sound to respond to an owner who has called her or to greet another cat she knows well.
Rare	Hiss or growl	"Go away!"	A cat can spit or make a growling sound to ward off an intruder or another cat she doesn't like. The aim is just to intimidate the other animal; the cat will go no further if the intruder retreats.
	Ow	"Ouch!"	This is the sound a cat makes instinctively when a human steps on her tail or another cat nips her. If you hear your cat make this sound, be sure to check she's OK.
It depends on the cat	Trill	"Excellent!"	These are the little sounds that some cats use to express their pleasure at the sight of a full bowl or after capturing their prey.
	Mew	"It's right there!"	This is a cry of excitement or frustration cats make when they see an insect or bird that's too far away to catch.
	Chattering	"Check me out!"	Made by a sexually active male or a female in heat to attract a mate, this yowling sound can be very loud. Males also use it competitively with rivals.
	Exhale	"And... relax."	This is a small miaow of relief that some cats make after a moment of particular tension or concentration.

HOW TO SPEAK CAT

CRYING AT NIGHT

"Night-time vocalization" is lower-pitched than the yowling sounds that a cat would make during courtship rituals. You need to look for the cause and deal with it quickly.

WHAT IT MEANS

If your cat is aged thirteen or over and she starts crying at night then you should take her to the vet as she could be sick.* Younger cats also sometimes cry at night, but this is not a cause for concern. It's likely that they're simply letting off steam or asking for something. But it can cause some disturbance to you or your neighbours.

**Your cat may also be crying during the day, but no one's around to notice, or the sound is drowned out by other noises.*

1

Characteristics of night-time vocalization

This tends to be a low-pitched, noisy monotone. The cat may seem to be making this noise without any particular aim, but it should alert you to possible health problems if they're older.

Like a wolf
There is no precise definition of night-time vocalization but cats often do it while looking at a fixed point. The sound is not dissimilar to a wolf's howl.

2

Young cats are fine

A young male cat may sometimes miaow at night, but that's probably just to encourage his owner to play (see page 37). From the age of thirteen, night-time vocalization needs to be taken seriously.

How long will it last?
As night-time vocalization has no precise purpose, nothing specific sets it off or stops it.

3

Treating the root cause

If whatever your cat is suffering from is diagnosed and treated, the night-time vocalization should stop. But some conditions, such as neurodegenerative diseases, are incurable. In these cases, a vet will be able to prescribe tranquillizers or sleeping pills for your cat to reduce her distress.

Useful information
You'll make your vet's life easier if you record the frequency of your cat's nocturnal vocalization. Even better, make a video clip of her doing it.

READ MY FACE

Cats have a large repertoire of expressions, ranging from affection to challenge. If your cat slowly blinks while she's watching you, she's displaying her attachment to you.

DON'T EXPECT SMILES

Cats feel no need to exhibit the equivalent of a smile, since they're naturally solitary creatures. This doesn't mean that cats who are friends don't show mutual trust with their body language or faces. They do! And they'll also sometimes act threateningly if they want to ward off an intruder.

Your cat will occasionally make a face that could be mistaken for a smile. This is the so-called flehman response,* which she uses to analyse pheromones in her surroundings.

**As when a cat draws back her upper lip and takes in air through her mouth to smell catnip, for example, or another cat's rear.*

1

Reading her face

It might seem as though cats are not very expressive animals. But our feline friends actually say a thousand and one things with their eyes and ears.

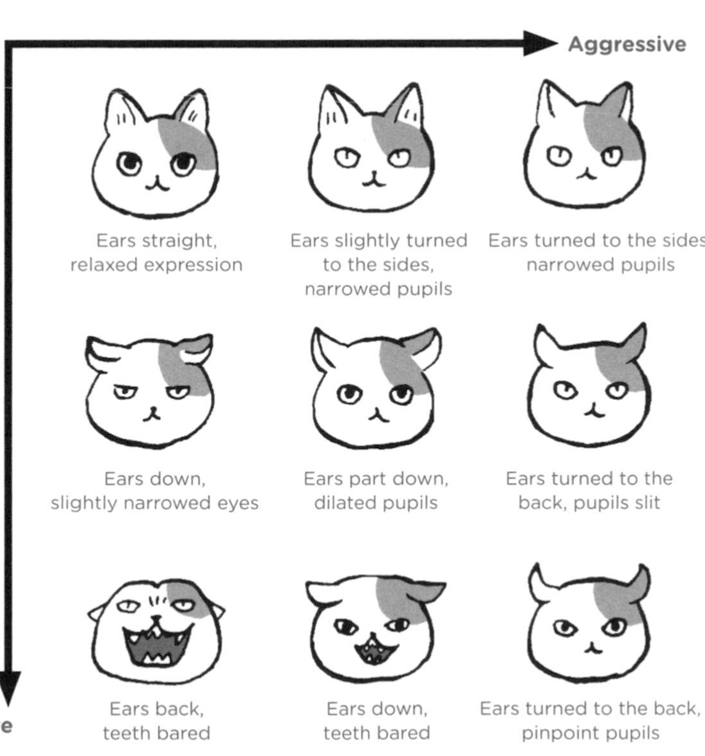

2

Reading her ears and whiskers

The ears of a relaxed cat will always be upright. Likewise, nice straight whiskers are a sign your cat is happy and healthy. If they're droopy, she's probably in a bad mood or under the weather.

Other body language
Cats can express affection with slow blinks or by licking the face of their favourite people.

HOW TO SPEAK CAT

BASIC BODY LANGUAGE

Domestic cats are relaxed most of the time. Get to know your cat's normal postures so that you can easily detect any change that may be a sign of illness.

GETTING TO KNOW YOUR CAT'S BODY LANGUAGE

Feral cats need to find their own food and protect themselves from predators, which means they're perpetually on the alert.

But domestic cats are free of such worries and live in a safe environment, which is why they so often look so relaxed. Nonetheless, they do sometimes appear restless because of illness or because someone they don't know has come into the home. It's a good idea to get to know your cat's normal body language so that you can easily identify any unusual behaviour.

1

Arched back to look impressive

To scare an enemy, a cat will try to make herself as imposing as possible by making her fur stand on end and presenting herself in profile. Sometimes she'll be confident of her superiority – at other times she'll be bluffing...

Don't get involved
When a cat's in this state, she's geared up to fight, so there's no point trying to calm her down. Just give her a bit of time.

Watch carefully
If you try to touch your cat when she's distressed, she may attack you. It's best to leave her in peace.

2

She makes herself small when she's scared

When a cat's scared by a loud noise or a stranger in the house, she'll try to curl up with her tail between her legs. This is her way of showing a potential enemy that she means no harm. But if she feels cornered, she may attack.

Don't disturb a lounging cat
When a cat's in one of these positions, she's almost certainly sleepy, so it's best to leave her in peace.

3

Favourite relaxation positions

She's only truly relaxed when she's either curled up in a ball, stretched out on her back or sleeping on her side with her paws stretched out.

STRETCHING IT OUT

In yoga, "the cat" is a stretching pose, probably because cats are so fond of stretching. When they're doing so, they're not asking you for anything: a stretch is just a stretch.

A NICE RELAXING STRETCH

Since animals express themselves mainly through body language, humans tend to analyse their pets' every little gesture. In reality, cats don't stretch to tell you they want something, but simply to get the blood flowing to their legs. All the same, it's hard not to empathize with a stretching cat, knowing how much we enjoy a good stretch ourselves.

1

Improving the circulation

If a cat remains in one position for too long, her body may get stiff and her blood flow slow. Stretching gets rid of the stiffness in her legs and gets her blood pumping.

I'm going to get up!

No risk of pressure sores
Even if a cat stays in exactly the same position for hours, her light bodyweight means there's no risk of pressure sores.

2

Changing tack

Cats stretch when they've had enough of playing or have just woken up; in other words, when they want to move on to a different activity. In this, they're like us...

What's that?

Doing stretches
Stretching can be a way of warming up before a play session.

3

Stretching and osteoarthritis

If your cat stops stretching in the normal way, she may be suffering from joint pain. Osteoarthritis mainly affects older cats, so it's worth keeping an eye on how often your cat stretches as she gets older.

That hurts!

Painful paws
If your cat starts walking strangely and stops jumping and climbing, she's likely to be trying to protect a painful joint. In which case, film her before taking her to the vet, as this will greatly assist diagnosis.

PURRS AND ASKING FOR AFFECTION

Adult cats love rediscovering their inner kitten and asking for affection from their owners. Learn how to respond to their requests.

THE MYSTERIES OF PURRING

In general, cats purr when they're in a good mood or if they're looking for a cuddle. As kittens purr when they are suckling, this particular sound is thought to be a way of expressing a general sense of wellbeing.

Sometimes cats purr when they're unhappy too (the sound may be slightly different from their usual purr), which just goes to show how mysterious purring still is.

How the sound is produced is another enigma, though it's thought to originate in vibrations of the diaphragm. Whatever its origin, it always delights cat owners to hear their contented pets make such a calm, lovely sound.

1
Purring and suckling

Almost from birth, kittens begin purring while they're suckling from their mother. It's probably their way of expressing satisfaction.

Purr, purr, purr...

Purring for milk
It's believed that kittens' purring may encourage the mother's lactation.

I feel good...

2
Happy sounds

Cats generally purr when they're being stroked. But the frequency and intensity of the purrs will vary from cat to cat.

Cuddles!
If your cat starts purring on your lap, she's feeling affectionate. Try not to move too much and don't be stingy with your attentions.

3
Purring at the vet's

The most laid-back cats can keep purring happily even at the vets. But more often cats who purr there are doing so because they're in pain and this purr is different from their normal one.

Purr
Purr
Purr
What you looking at?

Healing technique
It's been claimed that injured cats purr so that the vibrations they generate strengthen their bones and speed up the healing process.

HOW TO SPEAK CAT

RUBBING UP

A cat uses her head and tail to leave her scent all round her territory and as a form of reassurance.

GREETINGS AND TERRITORIAL MARKING

Cats have scent glands on their heads* and at the base of their tails, which they use to leave their scent on other cats when they rub heads in greeting. They would do the same with their owners if their heads were within reach, but instead make do with rubbing themselves against the arms and legs of the people they live with.

Cats also use scent to mark their territory. This is why they love curling their tails around the furniture at home.

**These are on their foreheads, under their chins, around their mouths and at the base of their ears.*

1
Bunting

As most of her scent glands are on her head, a cat will greet her friends with a head rub - bunting - in which they exchange scents with each other. She does the same with humans, using her head to transfer her scent.

Signs of friendship... and ownership
Your cat scent-marks you by rubbing against you. This means you belong to her!

2
Constant rubbing

As scents are more volatile than urine, scent-marking is a never-ending process.

Over and over
Some cat owners' furniture gets "polished" by the constant rubbing of their pets.

3
Self-assertion

When several cats live together, males show a stronger desire than females to mark their territory and therefore to rub everywhere. This can turn into a nightmare if the cats don't get on well together.

HISSING AND INTIMIDATION

If your cat hisses too often, she's probably finding her environment stressful.

A WAY OF AVOIDING FIGHTS

Hissing is a way of intimidating an adversary, whether it is another cat, a human, a dog or even an inanimate object that arouses your cat's suspicion. Although this is often seen as aggressive, in fact its purpose is to ward off the adversary and so avoid conflict.

If it works, your cat will be relieved she doesn't need to fight. But if your cat hisses too often, it's a sign of stress, so you should rethink her domestic environment and make sure that she has a cosy place to retreat to.

Fear of the unknown
A cat may consider any strange person or animal who comes into her home – her territory – as a threat and spit at them. Fear may also make her hiss when she's in an unfamiliar place, such as the vet's surgery.

1

Defensive, not aggressive

A cat who spits at a stranger is telling them not to encroach any further on her territory.

2

More scared = more hissing

A cat who hisses too often is a stressed cat. To reduce her anxiety, you could give her a place she can retreat to and feel safe, even when you have visitors.

Don't try to calm her
A hissing cat is a cat ready for a fight, so don't approach her or you could get a swipe from her claws.

Territorial battles
When two cats spit at each other and neither backs down, a fight will ensue and the loser will be banished from the disputed territory. In the wild, he'd then have to seek another territory or face starvation.

3

Street cats and territory

Fights often break out over the demarcation line between two cats' territories. Young male cats often start these scraps in a quest for females or more territory.

WHAT THE TAIL SAYS

Tail movements can tell you a lot about what your cat is feeling. If she comes towards you with her tail upright and held high, she's looking for a cuddle.

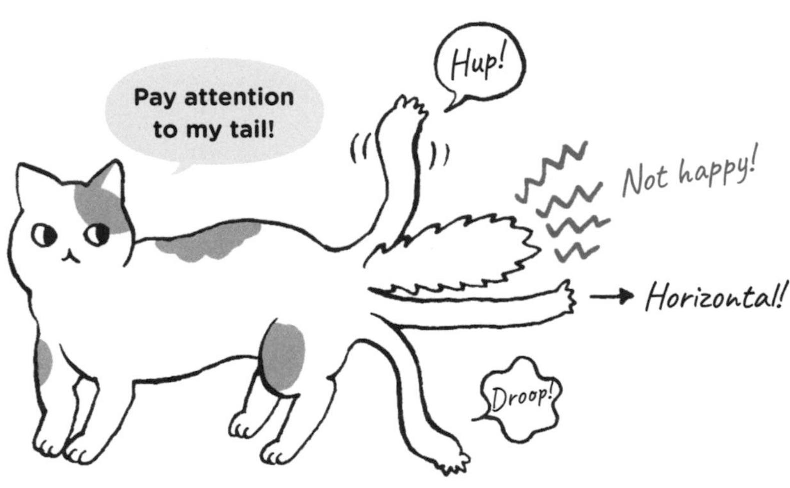

READING YOUR CAT'S TAIL

By paying attention to your cat's tail, you can read her like a book. Your pet cat can express a multitude of emotions depending on whether her tail is extended, curled, waving or puffed – wild cats do the same thing. It's highly likely that this means of expression comes from their shared ancestors.

Dogs also use their tails to express their feelings, but bear in mind that the same posture can have a completely different meaning in dogs and cats.

A cat's tail and her mood

A cat's tail has eighteen or nineteen bones and twelve muscles, so she can move it in very subtle ways to express sophisticated feelings.

Friendly, satisfied	Happy	Aloof	Angry
When her tail is upright, a cat is saying hello.	The tail is quivering slightly.	The tail is vertical but swishing from side to side.	With a tail puffed like this, a cat is trying to intimidate an adversary.
Unconfident	**Unsure**	**Calm**	**On alert**
The tail is upright but the tip is curled.	While the cat is watchful, her tail is slightly higher than horizontal.	A cat with a horizontal tail is completely relaxed.	The tail is lowered and slightly outstretched.
Potentially aggressive	**Submissive**	**On alert or interested**	**Annoyed**
The tail is pointing down and the cat is in attack mode.	The cat is scared and is trying to make herself small. her "hidden" tail is a sign of submission.	The end of the tail is flicking as the cat focuses her attention on something.	The tail is swishing from side to side and may even be striking the ground.

WINDING DOWN WITH A LICK-BATH

The ritual of grooming improves a cat's wellbeing. Cats may even lick their bodies to relax and deal with stress.

GROOMING AND THE SEASONS

Just as humans change their wardrobe with the seasons, cats regularly renew their coats.

The change of season is a good time for cats, whether long- or short-haired, to shed and regrow their coats. But for domestic cats, who are less exposed to seasonal variations in temperature, this cycle is not so noticeable as it happens throughout the year.

Even though your cat knows how to groom herself, it's still worth brushing her (see pages 90–91), as this will not only help get rid of dead hair, but also improve her blood circulation and the appearance of her coat.

1
Basic upkeep: brushing

Your cat knows how to groom herself, so all you need to do is give her a helping hand with brushing. Use a dematting comb and a carding comb for long-haired cats and a rubber grooming brush for short-haired ones.

Brushing and dead hair

The first time you brush your cat, you may be surprised by how much hair she sheds. But don't worry! All this hair is dead and in time would have fallen out naturally.

A shared moment

As brushing improves a cat's circulation, it has similar beneficial effects to a massage. It also enables you to share a moment of togetherness with your pet.

2
Daily brushing for long-haired cats

Daily brushing is vital for long-haired cats to stop knots and burrs forming in their fur, which can lead to skin infections.

3
Excessive grooming

Sometimes a cat will lick herself to calm herself down, for example after attempting a jump that doesn't come off. But if she licks herself too often, your cat may be distressed and engaging in the feline equivalent of human nail-biting.

The hidden meaning of excessive licking

An anxious or stressed cat can find temporary relief through licking. This is known as a substitution activity. It may also mean they have an allergy, or parasites.

FELINE BEHAVIOUR

UP TO SCRATCH

Cats scratch to get rid of the dead outer layer of their claws so that they stay sharp. They keep their claws retracted most of the time and only get them out when they need to.

SCRATCHING IS INNATE AND VITAL

Cats need to scratch because sharp claws are essential for catching their prey. Scratching also enables them to mark their territory by leaving their olfactory signature on things they've scratched, and may also help alleviate stress and frustration. So, it's an innate feline behaviour that you shouldn't try to stop.

To protect your furniture, get your cat a nice scratching post or horizontal scratching pad, depending on what she seems to prefer.

1

Scratching to mark territory

When a cat scratches something, she leaves the scent of her claws and paws on it to mark her territory. To make herself appear bigger than she really is, she'll stand on her hind legs to scratch higher up.

Big cats do it too

Big cats, especially panthers, also like to scratch as high up a tree as possible.

But not with back legs

Because of the structure of the back legs, cats can't sharpen their back claws. They don't need to be sharp anyway, as they aren't used to catch prey and wear down naturally.

A necessary evil

It's your responsibility to protect your furniture with covers and provide a sufficiently attractive alternative for your cat to scratch on. When you buy her a scratching post, place her forepaws on it and rub them gently on it to mark it with her scent.

Protecting against scratching

You can protect your furniture and walls with anti-scratch panels made from acrylic resin. Their smooth surface will discourage your cat from sharpening her claws on them.

Arthritis and scratching

If you notice your cat scratching her claws less often or see that the claws themselves are less sharp than usual, pay close attention to how she's walking and sitting. She might be suffering from arthritis.

Older cats' claws

Elderly cats find it harder to retract their claws, so they catch more easily on carpets and curtains. As this can be dangerous for them, get their claws clipped more often.

FELINE BEHAVIOUR

KICKING BACK

Beware of kicks from your cat's hind legs! She uses them to make gravity-defying jumps, so they're very powerful.

ALL PART OF THE HUNT

Cats are born hunters and even domesticated ones can't resist chasing after a moving target and trying to catch it. It's the same instinct which makes them use their hind legs to kick a toy or their owner's hand.

It might seem like just a game to you, but it's a serious training exercise for hunting to your cat, who could get carried away and end up biting you or kicking you without restraint.

1
Designed for kicking

When she jumps or climbs a tree, a cat uses her rear legs like springs - that's how powerful they are. Her front legs meanwhile support the weight of her head and body while she's doing this.

Reduced strength
If your cat lacks strength in her rear legs it could be because she's suffering from arthritis, nerve damage or a fractured bone.

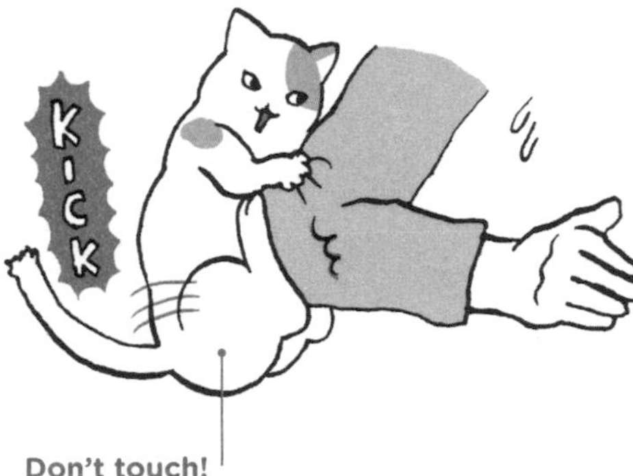

Don't touch!
Cats don't like their rear paws being touched (see page 113). Some aren't keen on their forepaws being touched either.

2
Hunting - a serious business

If your cat kicks you with her rear legs, she's practising her hunting skills. Even when she's training with a human, she's not going to hold back.

3
Let the soft toy have it

If your cat hurts you with her rear legs during a play session, stop the game and give her a soft toy instead. It's important you don't scold her as she's only obeying instinct. Let her take out her frustration by attacking her toy.

Front and back
The bodyweight is supported by the forelegs, but the hind legs are much more powerful.

FELINE BEHAVIOUR

NIPPING AND THE HUNTER'S INSTINCT

Your cat may confuse your finger with a toy during a play session and bite you. To teach her to be more careful, walk away from the game.

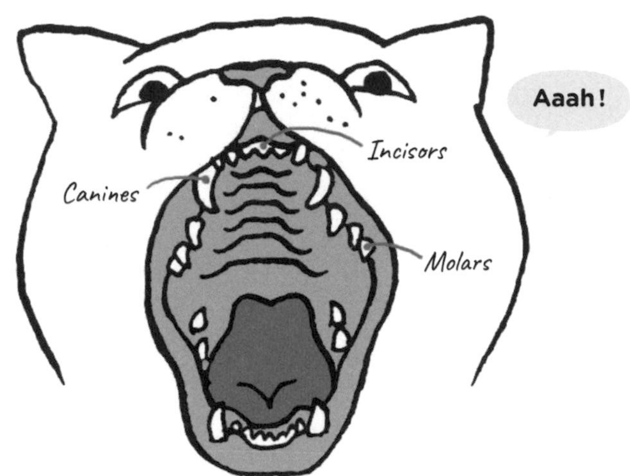

TYPICAL CARNIVORE TEETH

Around the age of four months, a kitten starts to lose her milk teeth, which will be replaced over the course of 2–3 months.

In the wild, cats sink their powerful canines into their prey, tear the flesh from the bone with their incisors, then rip it apart with their molars.

Cats don't need to chew their food because they are so good at digesting meat, their main food source.* It's worth noting that dry food is designed to be eaten as it is, so even if your cat loses all her teeth, she can still keep eating it.**

**Cats are pure carnivores, so meat is essential to their diet.*

***A build-up of dental plaque can lead to tartar forming, which can allow bacteria to get into the gums, so good oral and dental hygiene is important.*

1
Kittens nipping

Kittens bite everything they come across as hunting practice. Because they lack experience, they can sometimes bite really hard. Kittens from the same litter start play-fighting at six weeks. They gradually learn to inhibit their bite through being told off by their siblings when they nip them too fiercely.

Ankle-nipping

Perhaps your cat has nipped you on the ankle as you've passed her by. From a cat's vantage point, your ankle looks like moving prey and the urge to pounce may be irresistible.

Educating a kitten

You must avoid scolding a kitten who bites, but that doesn't mean you should let her get into bad habits. If your kitten bites you, walk away so she learns that this behaviour means the game or the cuddles stop immediately.

2
Biting and education

If your cat bites, ignore her. When she sees your lack of reaction, she'll get tired of biting. And when you play with her, use something such as a feather toy to avoid being nipped accidentally.

3
Reasons for biting

It's also important to know what is making your cat bite, apart from simple hunting practice. When you know why she's doing it, you can take steps to prevent it.

Look for the cause

Your cat may be feeling stressed or experiencing pain. She may also be unable to bear you touching a part of her body, such as her paws or claws. Only by paying attention to how she acts every day will you understand her behaviour.

FELINE BEHAVIOUR

GETTING TERRITORIAL

As cats are solitary creatures, each individual needs to mark its territory clearly so that other cats don't encroach on it. Territorial marking is a natural behaviour.

THREE TYPES OF TERRITORIAL MARKING

Cats mark their territory by leaving the smell of their body or urine in strategic places.

The most powerful mark is a spray of urine, usually made by uncastrated males. As the aim is to declare loud and clear whose territory it is, it smells much more strongly than normal urine and is sprayed over a larger area. Castration is a good way of completely or partially stopping this unwelcome behaviour.

The two other ways that a cat might mark out his territory are by scratching (pages 60–61) or rubbing himself against things (pages 52–3).

1
Go high

Whatever method a cat uses to mark his territory, he will always try to leave his scent as high up as possible to make other cats think he's bigger than he really is.

Pungent
A jet of urine sprayed by a male to mark his territory smells so strongly that even a human's poor sense of smell can tell it's different from normal urine.

It keeps on coming
If he isn't castrated, a male cat will keep up his daily spraying.

2
Girls are different

Female cats are generally less territorial than males. As long as they have enough food, they won't try to defend their territory against the odds. For males, it's about trying to lay claim to as many females as they can.

3
Castration as the remedy

A young male is ready for castration at four months, so long as he is a normal weight. If he's already got into the habit of urine-marking, castration may not stop this behaviour. Females rarely engage in urine-marking, so spaying has no impact. But for all cats, it's still best to neuter before puberty, at four months.

Don't scold him
Urine-marking is natural behaviour for a male cat, so there's no point telling him off for it. Castration is the only solution.

FELINE BEHAVIOUR

A CAT'S POSE REVEALS HER STATE OF MIND

Cats express their mood by the way they sit or recline. For example, a cat lying on her back with her stomach exposed feels completely secure and safe.

MANY DIFFERENT WAYS OF SITTING

You can tell how relaxed a cat is from how she's sitting.

In the wild, cats are always on the look-out for a predator appearing from nowhere. That's why they always sit in a way that would allow them to take flight quickly.

But domestic cats are protected from external threats and often show how relaxed they are by lying on their back or sitting with their paws crossed.

Some cats show great originality in the way they loll about, but if your cat suddenly starts sitting in strange positions, watch out as she may have joint problems...

1

Hind legs stretched out

By keeping her hind legs stretched out while she's sitting, a cat is ready to get up and go instantly. A cat in this position is not completely relaxed.

Scottish Fold cats
Scottish Folds often sit with their hind legs stretched out. This breed has a specific cartilage problem which means they can't bend their hind legs.

2

Totally relaxed

When a cat sleeps on her back with her stomach exposed, or sits with her paws crossed, she is completely relaxed.

Ultimate proof of relaxation
A cat's stomach is the most vulnerable part of her body. If she exposes it, that means she trusts you completely.

3

Joint problems in older cats

If you notice your cat's sleeping in a different position from usual, she may have trouble with her elbow or knee joints or her hips.

Arthritis in older cats
Up to 70% of cats older than twelve are likely to suffer from arthritis. If you think your cat may be one of them, talk to your vet, who will be able to recommend pain relief and any changes in the layout at home to make life easier for her.

FEELINE BEHAVIOUR

SOMETHING IN THE WAY SHE MOVES

A cat's gait is another way to work out her mood.

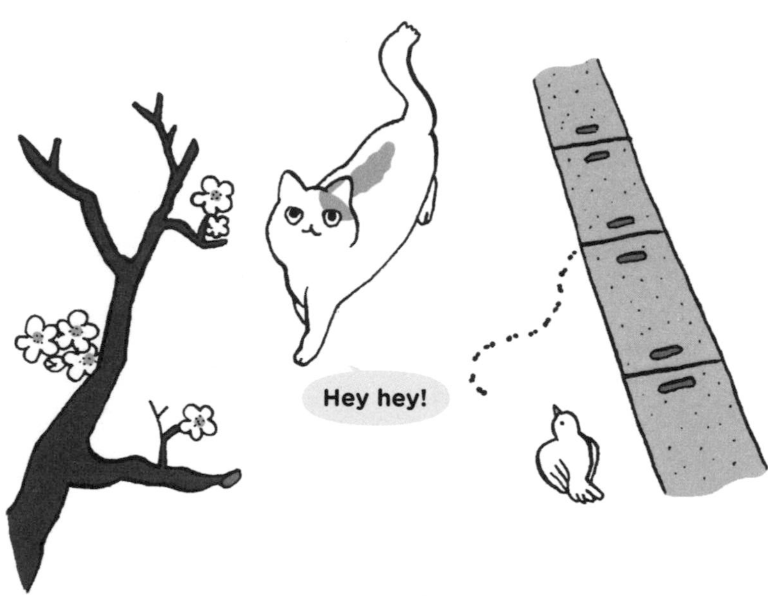

WALK THIS WAY

If your cat looks like she's trotting, nose and tail up, that means she's in a very good mood.

Conversely, if she's dragging her feet then she may be out of sorts. By getting to know your cat's "normal" way of walking you will be able to tell if anything changes or seems to be amiss.

While we're on the subject, did you know that cats are "digitigrade" animals? This means that they walk on their toes. It's the same for dogs!

1

Staying close to the ground

Cats keep their bodies low when they're on their guard or in hunting mode. If they're stalking, they get their tummies as close to the ground as possible, then pounce at just the right moment.

Why the wiggle?
A cat may wiggle her rear end while watching her prey. This movement is a sign she's trying to contain her impatience until it's the right time to strike.

2

Unusual gait suggests pain

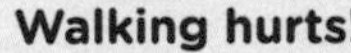

A healthy cat distributes her weight evenly on all four limbs as she walks. If she's limping or refusing to put one leg down, she's in pain.

Other signs of pain
If a cat seems to be protecting one leg as she walks, that means it's causing her pain. Usually, she won't let you touch this leg, so she will need to be taken to the vet.

3

Head down, walking on her hocks

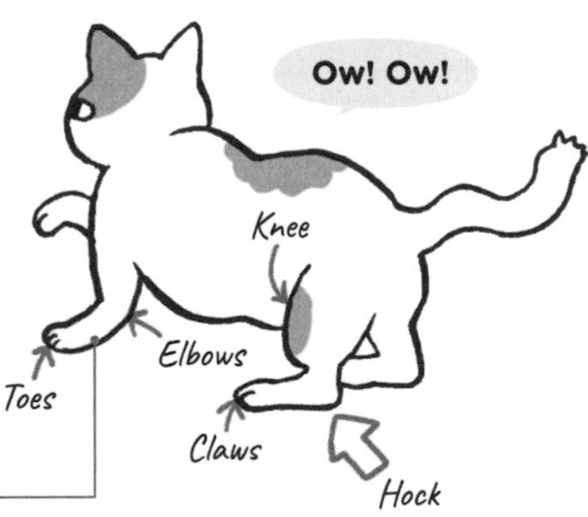

If your cat walks in this "low-slung" style and is not on guard or hunting, she's probably ill or in pain.

Diabetes risk
If your cat walks on her hocks, she may have diabetes. The "hock" is found on a cat's hind leg – it's simply the spot where the bones jut outwards.

FEELINE BEHAVIOUR

THE HIGH LIFE

Your cat feels at home when she's perched up high. Just make sure she doesn't take a tumble.

IT'S IN THE GENES

In the wild, cats love a high vantage point where they can detect their prey more easily and feel safe from predators.

This sense of wellbeing when high up has been passed on to domestic cats, and it's quite common to see them fighting for top spot in a cat tree, for example. The strongest cat will win, though that's not necessarily the one at the top of the social hierarchy.

If you want to set up a cat tree in your home, don't be over-ambitious – match the height of the tree to your cat's physical abilities.

1
A sense of balance and the righting reflex

A cat's "vestibular apparatus" (part of her inner ear) enables her to distinguish up from down if she's falling, and then position herself with paws downwards. Cats inherited this amazing talent from their distant tree-dwelling ancestors. It's a gift that also enables them to leap distances up to 2.5 metres.

Padded for a soft landing
The soft pads on a cat's feet, which we love so much to stroke, are in fact highly effective shock absorbers that she can use to ensure a soft landing when she jumps or falls.

Triple salto!

How to spot a fracture
If your cat is miaowing in an unusual way or is having difficulty moving, she may have fractured a limb.

2
Small falls still hurt

Falling off a sofa may seem like no big deal, but it can be. When a cat tumbles from a very low place, there's no time to turn around, so there's greater risk of a fracture.

3
Careful on the balcony

Even if your cat doesn't go outdoors, she may still have access to the balcony. If so, you need to take great care to avoid her falling because this can prove fatal – especially if you live on the fourth or fifth floor. From the sixth floor up, the risk of death decreases, as a quirk of physics means the speed of the fall tends to diminish. But whatever the floor, the risks are very real.

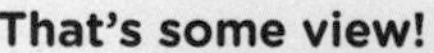

Make the balcony safe
If you want your cat to be able to go onto your balcony, you must install a grille or mesh that your cat can't slip through.

FELINE BEHAVIOUR

LOVE OF TIGHT SPACES

It's vital to provide your cat with a small hiding place where she feels safe. But if she refuses to come out of it, she may be unwell.

THE SMALLER, THE BETTER

Cats love hiding in narrow spaces, such as the gap between furniture or inside a chest of drawers. This is another instinct that comes from their wild ancestors, who made themselves as small as possible to feel safe from predators and allow themselves to relax. If the hiding place is also high up, your cat will be doubly delighted.

Even if your cat never goes out and is never exposed to danger, it's important to give her access to hiding places where she can sleep peacefully and take refuge when there are visitors around.

1

A place of her own

Your cat is perfectly capable of finding her own cosy hide-out, but you can encourage her by putting her favourite cushion somewhere high up.

Play tunnels and cardboard boxes
There are many cat accessories available which make a cat feel like she's in a den, but an ordinary cardboard box with a half-closed lid can be just as good.

2

Cat curiosity

Cats don't hide away just to get peace or because they're scared. Some of them do it out of curiosity, as part of exploring every corner of their environment.

It's a natural instinct
A cat's unconditional love of hard-to-get-to, narrow spaces is shared with her wild relatives, who love to be hidden from large predators.

3

A cat in hiding may be ill

If your cat remains in her hiding place, refusing food and not responding when called, she is ill and needs to go straight to the vet.

Just sulking?
Cats can refuse to come out of their hiding places because they're sulking. It's helpful to know your cat's character to avoid unnecessary worry.

FELINE BEHAVIOUR

WHY'S MY CAT VOMITING?

It's important to notice how often your cat is sick, so as not to miss signs of possible health issues.

BE AWARE OF THE TYPE OF VOMITING

Unlike humans, cats can vomit even when they're in good health. This is especially true of long-haired cats, who swallow strands of fur while grooming themselves and have to cough up the hairballs that form in their stomachs.

Cats that eat too quickly also tend to throw up, usually just after eating. This is because the food swells abnormally when it comes into contact with the gastric juices in the cat's stomach. To stop greedy cats regurgitating their food, they need to be encouraged to eat more slowly (page 28).

Although it may not be unusual for cats to be sick, it's worth paying attention to how often it happens. If it becomes more frequent, a trip to the vet is in order.

1

Four warning signs

① Your cat is vomiting more than once a week
② She's losing weight
③ She's off her food
④ She has diarrhoea

If at least one of these signs is present, you should take your cat to the vet.

What's she vomiting up?
If your cat is coughing up hairballs but has none of the symptoms listed above, there is no cause for concern. If you're not sure if what she's brought up is a hairball, show it to your vet.

Home-grown cat grass
Cat grass isn't a specific plant. It's a mix of grasses or cereals (such as barley) that your cat might like. You can buy a pot of cat grass for growing at home.

2

"Cat grass" helps with regurgitation

It may be helpful to give cat grass to cats who have difficulty bringing up hairballs. Eating the grass will stimulate the cat's digestive system and induce vomiting. It's dangerous for hairballs to remain stuck in the intestine, but normally they are eliminated by vomiting or excretion.

3

Short-haired cats

Compared to their long-haired cousins, short-haired cats swallow less hair when they groom, so they should be sick less often. If they're regularly bringing up hairballs, it suggests they're shedding too much fur.

If your cat can't be sick
If your cat is trying to bring something up, but can't, something has probably gone down the wrong way or got stuck in her throat.

WEIGHT GAIN AND WEIGHT LOSS

Cats can get overweight just like humans. If this sounds like your cat, it's time to talk to the vet.

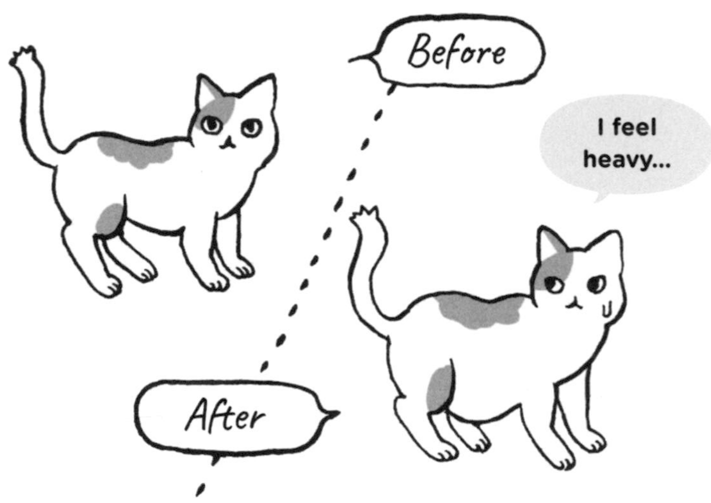

KEEP AN EYE ON YOUR CAT'S TUMMY

If your cat's stomach is the only part of her that's getting fatter, she may be ill. Take her to the vet without delay.

If her abdomen is partially swollen, she probably has a tumour, but it may not necessarily be malignant (cancerous, in other words).

If your cat's entire tummy is swollen but her legs and back look normal, she may be suffering from cancer or ascites (a build-up of fluid in the abdomen). Whichever it is, she urgently needs to be seen by the vet.

And of course, a swollen belly in an unspayed female cat may mean she's pregnant...

1

Judging your cat's body mass by eye

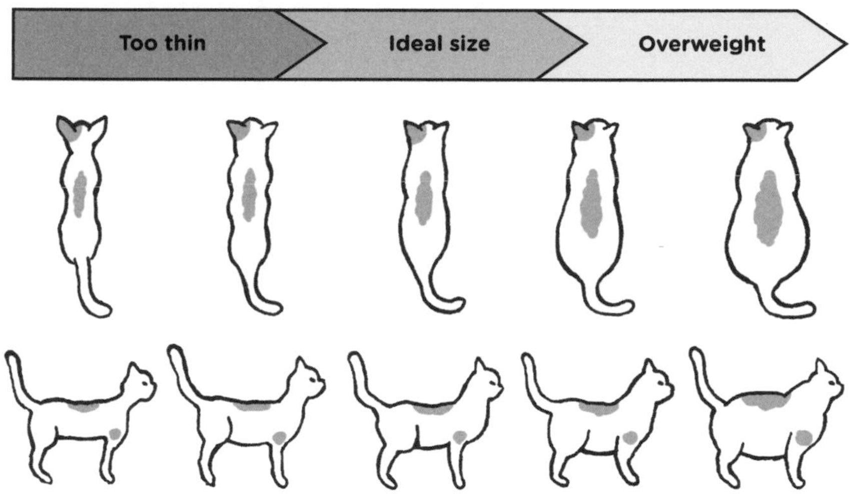

Your cat's ribs are visible, with angular haunches and a concave tummy. Her diet should be gradually increased.

You can feel where the ribs are, but you can't see them, as they're hidden beneath a thin layer of fat. In profile, your cat's haunches are angular and her tummy is concave.

Your cat's ribs are hard to feel with your fingers, as they're covered in a thick layer of fat, as are her haunches, stomach and legs. In profile, her stomach hangs down rather than being concave.

2

Abnormal weight changes

Remember that weight loss can be just as much of a warning sign as weight gain. Keep a close eye on any cat who loses or gains weight in just one body area (unlike in the illustrations above, where the weight is lost/gained overall).

Rapid weight loss or gain

If your cat ever loses 5% of her weight within a month, you need to monitor her carefully. If she's losing weight despite eating normally, she may be suffering from hyperthyroidism, a hormonal disorder which mainly affects cats over the age of eight. On the other hand, if your cat gains 5% additional bodyweight within a month then she's in danger of becoming obese, so cut back on her food and find ways to get her to exercise more.

FELINE BEHAVIOUR

WANTING TO COOL DOWN, EVEN WHEN IT ISN'T HOT

If your cat seeks out a cool place, she may be feeling unwell.

WHY CATS SEEK OUT COOL AIR

Cats like warm temperatures and when they're healthy, they don't tend to seek out the cold.

But when they're ill, their body temperature drops below its usual 38°C and the ambient temperature feels too hot to them.

It may also be the case that a cat who is unwell simply wants to be somewhere quiet, so she will seek out dark – and often cool – hiding places.

Whatever the reason, a cat who seeks out cool air is unwell and needs to be seen by a vet.

1

Cats move about because of the temperature

If it's hot weather and a room has got very warm, your cat will naturally want to go somewhere cooler. But if the room is ambient and she still wants out, keep an eye on her.

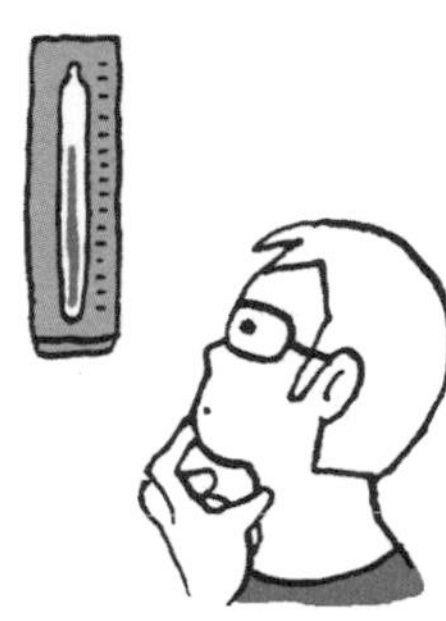

In winter

When the heating's turned up, your cat may feel too hot and want to leave the room. She'll be back when she starts to feel chilly. But if she remains in an unheated part of the house, monitor her health carefully.

2

Why does a sick cat want to be cool?

There are two reasons: either the ambient temperature feels too high as a result of her own body temperature falling, or she wants to hide away in a dark corner which just happens to be cool.

Finding cool places

An ill cat will settle down almost anywhere that's away from a heat source: in a corridor, on bathroom tiles or bare floorboards, in a wardrobe, etc.

Explain the situation

The vet will need to know where in the house your cat has been hiding and for how long.

3

Don't forget to visit the vet

When a cat who is already weakened by chronic illness or age refuses to come out of a cool place, it can be a warning sign. You should wrap her up in a warm blanket and take her to the vet.

EXTRA NOTES

2

GOING TO THE VET

Vets will often receive phone calls from cat owners saying, "My cat's been vomiting for three days and is off her food. Can I wait a bit longer before I bring her in?" If a family member were in the same situation, what would you do? You'd take them to the doctor immediately. **So don't be negligent just because it's a pet.** Treat her as you would a family member.

It is a very good idea to **take photos or videos showing what's wrong with your cat** so that you can show them to the vet when you go. These can be much more helpful than vague or confused explanations. Unless you are a health professional, it's easy to mix up symptoms such as coughing and sneezes.

It's also important to take pictures of your cat when she's well, as you can use them to compare her state of health at times when she's sick. A change in eye colour, for example, can easily and usefully be confirmed with an old photo; because you're with your cat so much of the time, you might find that you overlook things as obvious as this.

Many people like to research their cat's health online. But don't forget that some illnesses can prove fatal very quickly and require urgent treatment. **Don't rely solely on information you find on the internet and don't hesitate to seek specialist advice.**

CHAPTER

3

EVERYDAY CARE

RESPECT YOUR CAT'S ROUTINE

Cats are most active early and late in the day. They're also sensitive to the transition from day to night.

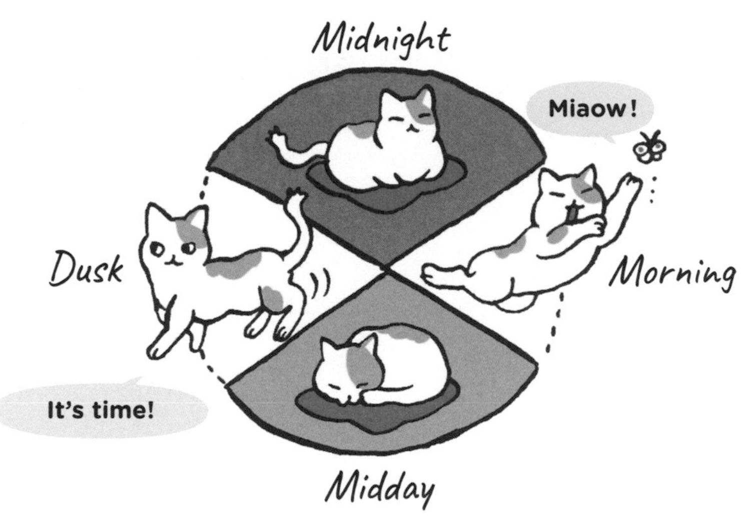

A GOOD ROUTINE MEANS GOOD HEALTH

Your cat really likes to know what time key events such as feeding will happen each day. A lack of stability can sometimes be a cause of illness so, to keep her healthy, it's a very good idea to stick to a routine.

To allow indoor cats to experience the shift between night and day, the ideal would be to provide lots of light during the day and then keep the light levels very low at night, simulating the effect of moonlight.

1
Know her toilet habits

Your cat will normally use her litter tray up to five times a day: once or twice to poo and two or three times to urinate. It's important that she wees about the same amount each time.

It won't
come out!

Urinary problems
If you notice that your cat has not urinated in the past twenty-four hours, her urethra may be blocked. Take her to the vet as soon as you can.

Bedtime
already?

2
Cats on heat

A female cat will usually come into heat as the days grow longer. But if she lives indoors and experiences darkness for more than fourteen hours a day, she won't come into season at all.

Becoming fertile
A cat's first season can start at five to six months for early developers, although it may not start till the cat is a year old. Indoor cats may experience as many as five or six cycles a year.

3
Erratic routines and health risks

If your cat seems out of sorts, sticking to a regular routine yourself could actually be a big help.

I want to
go to sleep!

Negative symptoms
When owners keep erratic hours, their cat may suffer from stress, loss of appetite and even diarrhoea and vomiting.

KEEPING YOUR CAT INDOORS

The outside world can quickly turn into a dangerous place for an indoor cat.

RISKS OF BEING OUTDOORS

Cat owners may choose not to let their cats roam about outside. Cats who are allowed out are often exposed to the risks presented by road traffic or can pick up diseases. They can also cause problems with your neighbours by defecating in their gardens.

It's worth bearing in mind that indoor cats tend to live longer (page 146) and enjoy better health than their free-range counterparts.

They do need fresh air and stimulation; a "catio" is ideal if you have a garden, or just a window where your cat can sit.

The dangers of traffic
A cat is often terrified the first time she sees a car or a bike.

1

Recognize the risks

Outside, your cat runs the risk of getting into a scrap with a cat who carries a disease, consuming pesticides if she lives near fields or ending up in some other trouble.

What on earth?!

Home sweet home!

2

Don't introduce her to the outside world

A cat who has been outside once will keep asking to be let out and it will be hard to deal with her frustration. In the long run, she will be more content if she lives a completely indoor life.

But isn't that cruel?
For most cats, the outside world is a source of stress as it exists beyond their own territory. That's possibly why most cats do not stay outside for long.

3

Escapologists

You can buy collars and harnesses intended for cats. But because cats are so supple, they're likely to be able to slip out of them. They also don't like being unable to escape if they see danger.

Walking the cat
Cats are not suited to being taken for walks because they are easily scared by loud noises and fast-moving objects.

Please release me!

LIVING TOGETHER

HOME ALONE

When you go out and leave your cat at home, you must make sure the temperature will remain at the right level and that she has food and water.

TWO DAYS TOPS

Leaving your cat home alone is not in itself a problem, as cats are naturally solitary animals, but it's best not to be gone for more than one night in case she experiences health problems. If a friend can drop by, that will provide reassurance. Don't forget to leave enough food and water, and make sure you remove any potentially dangerous objects before you go.

1 Human company

You could get a friend or a professional cat-sitter to look after your cat while you're away. This is essential for absences of more than one night. If your cat is not too stressed by a change of environment, you could also book her in to a specialist cattery.

Let the right one in
It's helpful if your cat already knows their "cat-sitter".

Hi there!

Tidy up before you go
Objects that your cat could break or scatter around should be put out of reach.

I'm peckish!

2 Increased portions

If you're travelling far, bear in mind that you might be delayed. It's a good idea to leave your cat more than the bare minimum of food.

3 Plenty to drink

It's essential to leave out plenty of water. Provide several different drinking places and make sure the containers can't be tipped over easily.

I'm really thirsty!

A stable bowl
In summer, if your cat knocks over her bowl and has no water, there's a risk of dehydration. In winter, she could catch cold by getting wet.

THE IMPORTANCE OF BRUSHING

A daily brush is a good idea during the moulting seasons (spring and autumn).

FUR MONSTER
Too much fur!

IT'S GOOD FOR A CAT'S HEALTH

Even if cats know how to groom themselves, some of them – especially flat-faced breeds – have trouble reaching their backs, so you need to help them get rid of dead hair.

Brushing will also prevent knots forming and help keep your house clean. Knots can cause dermatitis, and hairballs can cause an intestinal blockage if a cat swallows too many of them.

3

EVERYDAY CARE

1

How often to brush?

Long-haired breeds need a daily brush as they shed a lot. Short-haired cats can get by with a weekly brush.

Cats with undercoats

Thorough brushing is essential for cats with guard hairs (outer coats) and undercoats, which are particularly dense.

Watch out for static!

To avoid this problem, dampen the brush before you begin.

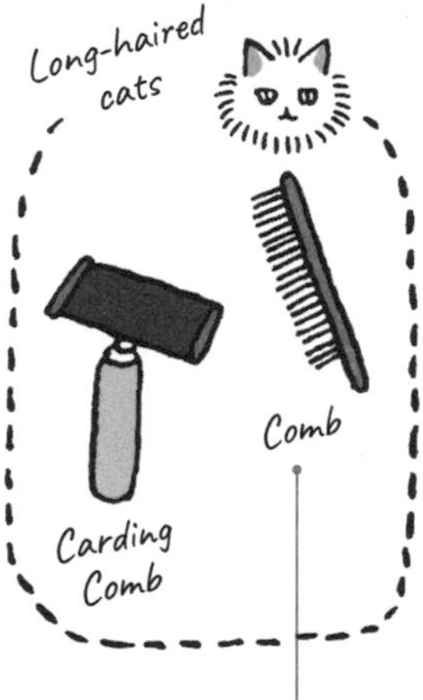

2

Different kinds of brush

Long- and short-haired cats need different kinds of brush. Always brush your cat following the direction of her fur, from neck to rump.

Brushing a cat's head

Use a comb to do this. For the fur under the chin, slide the comb from chin to chest, and for the cheeks and forehead, comb from the middle outwards.

3

Brushing unwilling cats

Many cats don't like their stomachs, tail and legs being touched. If yours is one of them, take your time. Don't try to brush all of her in one go; take it in stages.

Start them young

The best way to get your cat used to being brushed is to start as young as possible.

HEALTH CARE

DENTAL HYGIENE

Inflammation of the gums, caused by the build-up of dental tartar, can not only cause teeth to become loose, but also harm the heart and kidneys.

BRUSH THOSE TEETH

Cats rarely get tooth decay, but they do often suffer from dental problems caused by plaque build-up.

Once it has formed, tartar cannot be removed by brushing alone, so it's important to clean your cat's teeth regularly to prevent this happening. Daily brushing is especially recommended for cats fed on wet food, as its moisture content encourages plaque formation.

The best way to hold a cat when brushing her teeth is from behind, like in the picture above.

1

Toothbrush

You'll need a special small-headed, soft toothbrush and you should also use a special toothpaste for cats.

Instead of a toothbrush
For cats who resist having their teeth brushed, try a piece of medical gauze wrapped round your index finger and smeared with toothpaste.

2

How to begin

Start by smearing a little cat toothpaste on kitty's paws, for her to lick off. Then a few days later, use a cotton bud to rub it round her mouth. Eventually you will be ready for the toothbrush! If she is uncomfortable, go back to the stage before.

Brushing technique
Insert the brush gently into your cat's mouth and make small circular motions between the teeth and gums. You ideally want to do 30–45 seconds each side.

3

Pay attention to the molars

You need to brush the canines and molars well, especially the upper molars, which can easily become dirty. If your cat is cooperative, make sure you spend some time on this area of her mouth. Once tartar takes hold, cats need the same treatment as humans: ultrasonic removal, which your vet will be able to do, but it will not be cheap and a general anaesthetic will be necessary.

If your cat is reluctant
Don't feel you have to brush all her teeth in a single session.

HEALTH CARE

CLIPPING CLAWS

Even if your cat uses a scratching post, you should clip her claws regularly to prevent her from hurting herself.

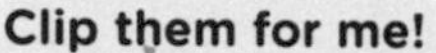

WELL-KEPT CLAWS

When your cat uses her scratching post, it's to sharpen her claws, not shorten them. If you don't clip the claws of an indoor cat regularly, they will keep growing and she may injure you or herself by accident.

So you should clip them at least once a month. If your cat won't let you do the full manicure in one session, aim to do one claw per day. And don't forget to give her a little treat to reward her for cooperating.

It's a little different for outdoor cats, as they need their claws for defence against possible attacks – so don't clip their claws.

1

Equipment

There are two sorts of clippers for claws: guillotine and scissor types. The scissor type is probably easier to use.

Never force your cat
If you force your cat to stay still while you cut her claws, she'll come to see this experience as an unpleasant ordeal and won't let you do it again.

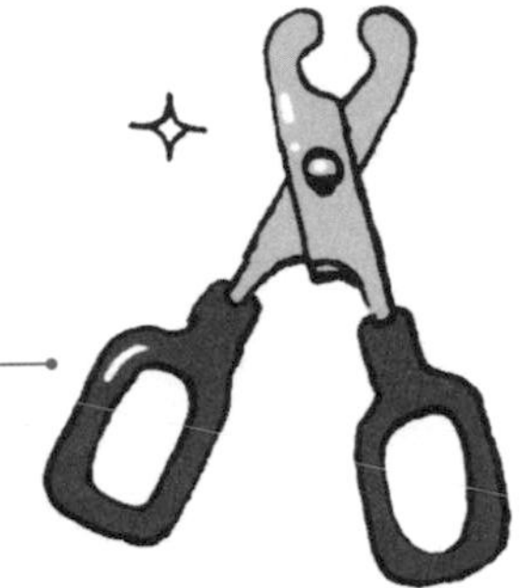

Two-person job
If you can enlist someone to help, one of you can hold your cat's leg while the other trims her claws. Don't hold the cat too tight or she's likely to struggle to get away.

2

Put her higher up

If you try to cut your cat's claws while she's on the ground, you'll be bent over and uncomfortable. It's easier if the cat's on a table.

3

Older cats' claws

As a cat gets older, her claws tend to become thicker and start to curl. If you fail to trim them, they can become embedded in her paw pads, which will prevent her from walking.

Cutting advice
Only trim the white end of the claws; it's best to ask the vet to show you how the first time. If your cat bleeds because you've accidentally nicked her flesh, staunch the bleeding by pressing a piece of gauze to it.

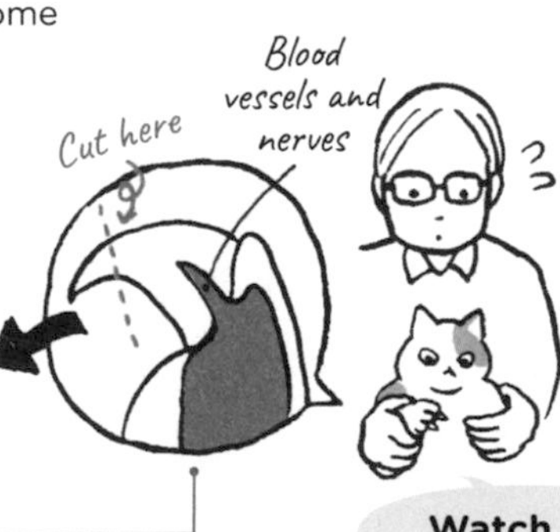

SHAMPOOING A LONG-HAIRED CAT

Before you attempt to shampoo your cat, make sure she's in good health and that she doesn't have a temperature (pages 80–81). Check too that her claws – and your nails – aren't too long.

CATS DON'T LIKE WATER

Domestic cats hate getting wet. If your cat doesn't go outside, then in theory she only needs to be shampooed if she is a long-haired breed.

Long-haired breeds have trouble grooming themselves as their tongue can't reach their skin. Their coats can quickly get dirty, with tangles in the fur.

1
Shampoo

Usually, short-haired cats don't need to be bathed, especially if they're brushed regularly. But long-haired cats need a bath once a month, which will also enhance the appearance of their coats.

Short-haired cats
Short-haired cats remove dirt by using their paws like a bathing mitt. You can use a warm, damp towel to clean their heads, the only area that their tongues can't reach.

I don't mind this!

How to bathe a cat
① Brush your cat
② Wet her body with warm water (around 38°C)
③ Wash her with cat shampoo
④ Clean her head with a sponge with a little shampoo on it
⑤ Rinse her thoroughly
⑥ Wrap her in a warm towel to dry her off
⑦ Dry her thoroughly with a hair-dryer, brushing her as you do so

If you notice at stage ① that your cat is shedding too much hair or has any broken skin, don't continue with the process.

2
Warm-towel clean for reluctant cats

If your cat finds a bath too stressful, you can clean her all over with a warm, damp towel.

Don't forget to brush
You should brush your cat before her bath to remove as much hair as possible. If you notice while doing this that she is shedding too much hair, or has any broken skin, consult your vet, who will be able to tell you if treatment is required before she can be shampooed.

3
Call in the professionals

If your cat won't even tolerate a warm towel, you could always take her to a professional groomer.

Shampooing kittens
The process of shampooing and drying is energy-intensive; kittens should be at least seven months old before they undergo it.

HEALTH CARE

NEUTERING MALES

After neutering, males are less inclined to mark their territory and they will become more biddable in character.

SOME BEHAVIOURAL ISSUES WILL STOP OVERNIGHT

If you have your cat neutered around the age of four months, this will significantly reduce his aggression towards other cats and his tendency to urine-mark his territory. The other advantage of neutering is that it removes the risk of genital infections.

This surgical process changes your cat's hormone balance and slows his metabolism, which may mean he puts on weight afterwards.

1

The best time for neutering

It's a good idea to have a male cat neutered around the age of four months, shortly before he reaches puberty. This means he won't develop a taste for marking his territory...

Around
four months

Ready for the op

Before cats of either sex are neutered, they should be aged at least four months and be a normal weight.

I'm ready
for love!

2

Later neutering means a chunkier tom

Around the age of three, intact males have a tendency to fill out and develop jowls.

Tom cats in love

Males start to rut when females are on heat. They show they are sexually mature by marking with urine, loud high-pitched miaowing and rubbing their genitals on everything and anything.

3

Under anaesthetic

Remember that any operation carried out under general anaesthetic does come with a risk of complications.

Have I put
on weight?

About the operation

Follow your vet's advice about whether your cat can eat before the operation. The surgery itself lasts only around a quarter of an hour and your cat should be able to come home the same day. Spaying females takes about half an hour and sometimes requires a day or two under observation afterwards.

SPAYING FEMALES

In almost 100% of cases, a female who has mated will become pregnant. If you don't want your cat to have kittens, you are strongly recommended to have her spayed.

BENEFITS OF SPAYING

This surgical procedure has several benefits for female cats. Not only will they cease to exhibit the behaviours associated with being on heat, but they will also avoid ovarian and uterine diseases, and they will be much less likely to get mammary tumours. The only downside to spaying is that female cats tend to put on weight after, so it's a good idea to review their food intake after the operation.

1

Ideal timing

It has been shown that if a cat is spayed before she goes on heat for the first time, it significantly reduces her risk of mammary tumours, so it is a good idea to have the operation done around the age of six months.

Ovaries?
Uteris?
???

About the operation
The procedure involves removing the cat's ovaries and uterus. As with the neutering of males, the vet will assess beforehand whether your cat is in the right condition for surgery. Follow the vet's instructions about how much to feed her before the operation. The cost is always higher than having a male neutered.

2

Hardly any change in appearance

Unlike males, the age at which female cats are spayed doesn't seem to affect their body shape, although they are likely to gain a little weight. Because they avoid the experience of going on heat, spayed cats seem physically less stressed than those who are intact.

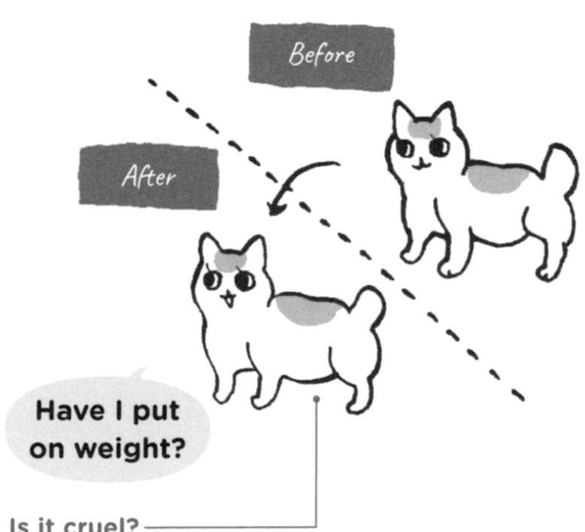
Before
After
Have I put on weight?

Is it cruel?
An intact female cat will constantly seek out males to mate with. Thwarting this desire by preventing her from mating would be crueller than spaying.

Not while she's on heat

A cat's uterus swells when she is on heat, so it's advisable to wait until this is over before having her spayed.

HEALTH CARE

A HAPPY, HEALTHY OLD AGE

You can lessen the impact of ageing by giving your cat food that's specially adapted for her age.

AGEING STARTS AT SEVEN

To slow down the ageing process, it's a good idea to give your cat high-quality food intended for her age. It's also important that she gets exercise that takes into account her physical condition: try getting her to play on the floor with her favourite toys.

Don't forget that your cat will be less able to climb and jump than before. Above all, it's important to spend time with her and to listen to her. You could also adapt her environment to bring down her stress levels.

1 The importance of shared moments

The older your cat gets, the more important it is to spend time with her to spot possible health problems.

Understanding her emotions

Cats are not naturally expressive creatures. But they do show their emotions through a subtle repertoire of postures, facial expressions and sounds.

2 The benefits of massage

Massage improves the blood flow, which helps the distribution of nutrients and oxygen throughout the body. If your cat has a nice time, it will also have a calming effect on her.

I feel good!

Don't hurt her

If your cat shows she is unhappy, reduce the pressure and massage her gently where she likes it.

3 Loss of muscle tone

From as early as the age of two or three, cats become more sedentary and they gradually start to lose muscle tone. To stop them gaining weight, it's a good idea to encourage them to move by initiating games.

Avoid vertical movement

Older cats lose their balance more easily. To avoid a fall from a height, it's better to get them to exercise at ground level, rather than encouraging them to climb.

EXTRA NOTES

3

NATURAL DISASTERS

In recent years, no part of the world has escaped natural disasters such as floods. To protect your cat if something dramatic occurs, you need to be prepared even in normal times.

When a natural disaster happens, cats have a tendency to panic and hide. To avoid having to hunt for your cat at a time of high stress, you could use a trick discovered by a man from north-east Japan, which was badly affected by an earthquake and ensuing huge tsunami in 2011. He had conditioned his cat to respond to an alarm he had at home by regularly sounding this alarm and then giving his cat treats. The day his town sounded the alarm to order a general evacuation, his cat responded and could be put into a pet carrier.

To prepare your cat for the possibility of staying in a communal shelter, it's important for her to get used to staying calm in a pet carrier (see pages 142–3) and not be scared by the presence of strangers.

It's also vital to have a mental list of cat-related items and documents that you may need if you are evacuated: cat food, feeding and drinking bowls, any medicines, health record with vet's details, litter tray, litter, etc. And don't forget to have your cat fitted with a microchip.

CHAPTER

4

MAKING YOUR CAT HAPPY

MAKING YOUR CAT HAPPY

CATS AND HUMANS

Cats are naturally attracted to people who are calm and quiet.

PLAYING IT COOL

All cat owners want their pets to love them, but sometimes we do things they don't like without realising.

Cats are not especially keen on being picked up or kissed. Nor do they like being called or handled without good reason. They hate people suddenly raising their voices. In general, they don't like their freedom of movement being curtailed or being disturbed while they're in peaceful mode.

1

Cat-friendly people

Cats are generally drawn to people who make gentle movements, talk calmly and have higher-pitched voices. If you don't fit that description, don't worry – by respecting their freedom and desire for independence, you can still make sure they'll get along with you.

Hold back
Cats don't like to be touched or stroked while they're eating or grooming.

2

Cat's-eye view

When you want to talk to your cat or stroke her, it's a good idea to get down to her level so as not to scare her.

3

Adapting to your cat's character

There are two sorts of cats: the affectionate ones, who like human attention, and the independent ones, who prefer to be left to their own devices. You'll be able to tell which category your cat is in by paying attention to her normal behaviour and her response when you stroke her.

Licking's a sign
If your cat goes off and licks the part of her body you've just stroked, she values her independence and wants to get rid of your smell as quickly as possible.

DO CATS HAVE PERSONALITIES?

You can try to get a sense of your cat's personality by watching out for expressions that reveal her character. A swishing tail or flattened ears are clear signs of her mood.

ALL SORTS OF PERSONALITY TYPES

Cats in the wild can hunt alone and don't need to live in packs. Because of this, their domesticated relatives tend not to interact with each other very much.

All the same, they do sometimes display empathy towards each other. For example, if your cat brings you something she's caught, she feels pity for what a terrible hunter you are, since you can't even catch a mouse.

1

A question of breeding

Slender, short-haired breeds such as the Abyssinian and the Russian blue are often lively. Long-haired cats, such as the Maine Coon and the Persian, tend to have more mild-mannered natures.

Always ready to play
Abyssinians are highly athletic and energetic, even into adulthood.

2

A kitten needs family

A kitten's ability to learn peaks when she's between three and seven weeks old. In this crucial character-forming period, she needs to be with her mother and siblings.

Too young to go it alone
Kittens should not be separated from their mothers before eight weeks. If they are, they will not be fully socialized, which will be detrimental to their future life.

3

It's in the genes

It's thought that kittens inherit their level of aggression from their father. Their mother can pass on psychological stress she suffered during pregnancy.

Effect on other pets
After giving birth, a cat will devote herself entirely to her litter. The cat owner is also going to be kept busy by the new arrivals. This situation can sometimes provoke jealousy from other animals in the house, so try hard not to neglect any of your pets.

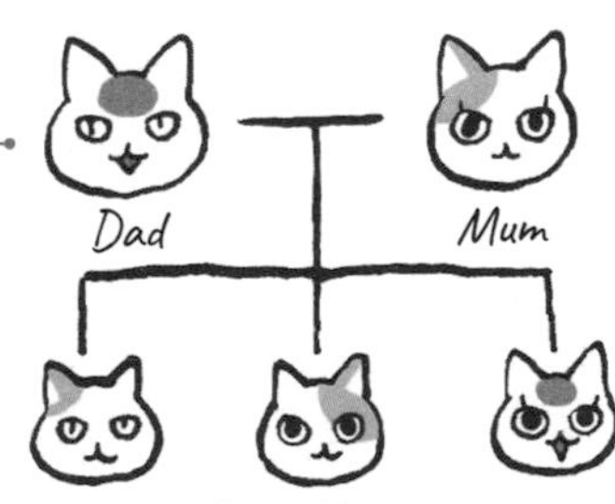

PLAYING WITH YOUR CAT

It's essential that you play with your cat regularly, even just for a short time. Young cats aged one or two need daily play. They'll continue to play as they age, though more intermittently.

PLAYING IS GOOD EXERCISE

You need to tailor the type and intensity of play to the age of your cat. When she's a kitten or still quite young, she needs a lot of play to develop both physically and mentally.

Play remains necessary to maintain muscle mass – try to come up with games suitable for your cat's age so that she stays active.

1
Cat and mouse

Shake an object in front of your cat, imitating the jerky movements of a prey animal running to and fro, pausing to catch its breath or trying to hide. Your cat will feel she's in full hunt mode.

Got you!

Choose toys that look like prey
A small soft toy attached to a string or a feather duster are good choices. The main thing is that the toy should resemble a mouse, insect or bird. A ball is another good choice: if you roll it quickly along the ground, your cat will try to pounce on it.

Playing with light
In this game, shine spots of light on the ground or a wall using a laser pointer, torch or mirror. Take care not to point the laser directly at your cat as this could harm her eyes, and give her a food reward at the end so she's not frustrated about not catching anything!

2
The appeal of new toys

It's worth giving cats new toys from time to time, to stimulate their curiosity.

Here it is!
There it is!

Give them space
Cats are animals that know their own minds. When they've had enough of playing, stop the game and let them have quiet time.

3
Useful precautions

Take care with toys which are small or soft, as your cat could swallow them or crunch them up; never leave her unattended with toys or string.

FAVOURITE SORTS OF CUDDLE

Your cat may suddenly bite you when you are petting her. If this happens, move away and leave her be.

SHARED MOMENTS

When you pet your cat, you're giving her pleasure. You can also use the opportunity of being close to her to make sure her body has no scratches or signs of hair loss. And don't forget that such special moments of togetherness also promote calm and relaxation in *you*. Take your time and savour these moments – they'll help you get to know your cat better.

1

Be more cat

One cat will lick another as a sign of affection. Your cat will love it if you stroke her in a way that imitates a cat's tongue, using the pad of your finger rather than the palm of your hand.

Cuddles = relaxation
Cuddling sessions with your cat have a calming effect. They also help build a solid relationship of trust with her.

2

Know when to stop

If your cat begins to swish her tail from side to side, or flattens her ears back, it's a sign she's almost out of patience, so leave her be.

When to avoid petting
Cats hate being interrupted when they're eating or grooming.

3

Where to stroke?

Cats generally like being stroked on the head, neck and back. But they won't be impressed if you try to touch their legs, tail or stomach, the most sensitive parts of a cat's body.

Winning their trust
Cats like people who speak softly and don't make sudden movements.

HOW TO PICK CATS UP

Remember your cat isn't a soft toy. Don't keep trying to pick her up if she clearly doesn't like it as you may end up making her resistant to any kind of handling.

SHARED MOMENTS

Most cats don't like being picked up: it makes them feel vulnerable and unable to escape if they need to. But the problem may sometimes be created by the way their owner picks them up or holds them. For a cat to feel safe in your arms, you need to hold her securely to you and support her rump. You will always have some reason to handle your cat, even if it's just to brush her teeth or groom her, so it's worth practising the best way to pick her up.

1

Call her first

Don't try to pick your cat up without warning; she's likely to struggle and run off. If you call her name, she'll learn over time to expect you to pick her up and will tolerate it more willingly.

You called?

Taking it slowly
If your cat doesn't like being picked up, get her used to being on your knee first by sitting on the floor and enticing her to come to you with a toy. When she's on your knee, lift her a little with your hands to get her used to being handled. The most important thing is to take it slowly.

2

The right way to hold a cat

Place one hand on your cat's body, behind her front legs, and the other under her rump. Quickly raise her to your body and hold her securely so that she feels safe.

Don't hold me too tight!

The key to her trust
When you're holding your cat in your arms, there should be no gap between your body and hers.

3

The wrong way to hold a cat

Never pick your cat up by the scruff of her neck. You should also avoid picking her up with her body dangling unsupported.

Put me down!

Learn to spot when she's had enough
Even if your cat allows you to pick her up, she'll soon want you to put her down again. As soon as she shows signs of impatience, lower her gently to the ground.

HOW TO TALK TO YOUR CAT

Use short words when you speak to your cat. Above all, speak softly.

SHARED MOMENTS

It's thought that cats have trouble making out consonants and can only distinguish vowels. That means they wouldn't be able to tell the difference between names like "Molly" and "Dolly", where the vowels are the same. Bear this in mind if you have several cats and are thinking about what to call them.

1

Short names are best

Pick a short and easy-to-remember name for your cat.

Top choices
Popular cat names include Bella, Lucy and Coco for females, and Oliver, Max and Rocky for males.

2

Keep your voice gentle

When you speak to a cat, talk softly and at a slightly higher pitch than normal.

What puts cats on edge
Cats don't like people who are brusque or who have booming voices, or constantly call them for no reason.

3

It's good to talk

Even if your cat can't understand what you're saying, talking to her helps strengthen your bond. Your voice is a welcome sound to her and helps her relax.

Some cats are just shy
Kittens are socialized between three and seven weeks old. If they're unable to become used to the presence of humans in this crucial period, they may remain wary of people their whole lives.

GIVING A FOOT MASSAGE

The pads of a cat's paws are soft to the touch; they don't have fur on them, as their function is to stop the cat slipping. Your cat will love it if you massage her paw pads.

FANTASTIC PAW PADS

A cat's paw pads act as shock-absorbers when she falls and they also enable her to slink closer to her prey soundlessly.

Hairs can grow between the individual pads of her front paws. If your cat is a short-haired breed, this shouldn't be a problem, but if she's long-haired she may slip on smooth surfaces, so you should trim them for her.

Interesting fact: the only place that cats sweat is through their paw pads.

ARE KISSES ALLOWED?

It's possible for cats to pass on some diseases to humans. Adults can understand the risks but children can't, so it's sensible to teach them to keep a certain distance from cats.

DON'T GET TOO CLOSE

Diseases that can be transmitted from animals to humans are called "zoonoses". Cats occasionally pass on diseases to humans via their intestinal worms. If a cat contaminated with these parasites licks its bottom during grooming, it can get the worm eggs around its mouth. If you kiss your cat or rub against her head, then you could be contaminated too. To tell if your cat has worms, all you need to do is examine her poo.

You are strongly advised to avoid this problem completely by regularly giving her parasite treatment.

NEW CAT ON THE BLOCK

The arrival of a new cat in the home can stress a cat who is already there. Before introducing a new cat, you should think carefully about whether your home is big enough to allow two cat territories, the additional cost implications and the right moment to bring the new cat back.

THE RIGHT COMBINATION

It's important to choose the right combination in terms of gender and family ties. The pairings that work best are a mother and one of her offspring, or two siblings, as these are all cats who have lived together since birth. If the cats have no blood relationship, a neutered male plus female pairing is usually the most successful, followed by two females.

1

Combinations to avoid

It's best to avoid keeping two tom cats as they're likely to clash over their territories. The combination of an old cat and a kitten is likewise not a good idea as the senior cat may be stressed by the newcomer's high energy levels.

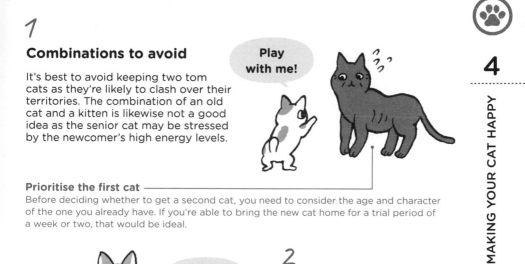

Prioritise the first cat

Before deciding whether to get a second cat, you need to consider the age and character of the one you already have. If you're able to bring the new cat home for a trial period of a week or two, that would be ideal.

Dogs mean stress

Dogs are not particularly stressed by the presence of a cat, but the opposite isn't true. Cats are instinctively scared of dogs.

2

Living with a dog

If the dog came first, the arrival of a kitten should be fine, but living with an adult cat can be a different matter. If the cat was first on the scene, introducing a dog can be problematic.

3

The seven-year rule

A cat's average life expectancy is fifteen years, so the ideal time to introduce a new cat is when your first cat is seven. When a cat dies, its owner is not the only one affected. Cats can also feel sorrow and pain, so it's important to reassure a bereaved cat with your presence.

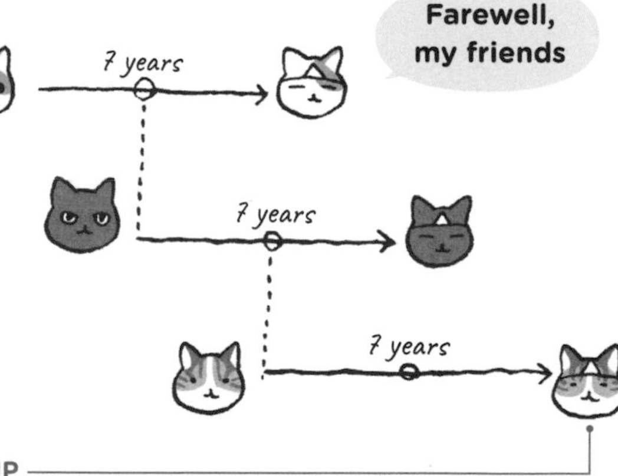

RIP

After your cat dies, you have three options: ① burial in a pet cemetery; ② burial in your garden; ③ cremation at the vet's.

EXTRA NOTES

4

WHICH TREATS ARE OK FOR CATS?

The food you feed your cat is designed to meet her nutritional needs. But many cat owners want to please their cats by giving them treats. If you do this, the best option is small pieces of chicken breast briefly blanched in water with no salt or flavourings added. You can also use cooked beef or pork (again with no salt added) but chicken is the top choice, as it contains more protein and less fat.

You also need to **pay attention to the quantity** you're giving her. A good rule of thumb is to ask yourself: could I eat a quantity twenty times what I am considering giving to my cat?

You might want to give her milk. The kind humans drink will give her a tummy upset because of the lactose, but you can buy special **cat-friendly milk** if you like!

CHAPTER

5

CREATING A CAT-FRIENDLY HOME

THE BASICS

When you're organizing your domestic space, consider your cat's basic needs.

ADAPTING TO YOUR CAT'S AGE

It's your responsibility to provide a safe, comfortable environment for your cat.

The floorplan opposite gives tips for how to arrange a home; the areas you need to pay particular attention to will vary depending on your cat's age.

Around the age of thirteen or fourteen, your cat's muscle mass will start to decline and she will have more difficulty jumping. At this stage, you should arrange things so that she can live her life at ground level. (Pages 138–9 include more advice on this.)

The ideal set-up

Cats are playful, inquisitive creatures. They'll happily nibble on electrical cables and sample the leftovers from your meals. Kittens are especially likely to do this. But whatever the age of your cat, don't leave clutter lying around, especially little things she might try to eat.

The cat's bed
This is where your cat will spend much of her time, so it must be as comfortable as possible. If the bed is too big, your cat will not feel sufficiently protected. For advice on finding the perfect bed, turn to pages 132–3.

Windows
Fit a grille or mesh on your window to prevent an indoor cat from escaping.

Cat tree
A cat tree will satisfy your cat's love of heights and she can practise climbing between levels. She would also enjoy a scratching post.

Floor covering
Fitted carpet or rugs reduce the risk of slips. But bear in mind that if your cat swallows pieces of polyurethane carpet backing, it could cause an intestinal blockage.

Litter tray
This should be near the place where your cat usually rests, but not close to her food (see pages 30–31 and 134–5).

Stairs
Cats older than thirteen or fourteen may fall down the stairs because they have become weaker with age. To prevent this, it can be a good idea to block access to the stairs.

Doors
Some cats hate air-conditioning. If yours is one of them, she should be able to leave an air-conditioned room when she wants, so always leave the door ajar.

Never leave dangerous objects lying around
Seemingly innocuous objects can be harmful if your cat swallows them, such as house plants, leftovers from your meals, sewing materials, medicines, ribbons, etc. (see pages 126–7).

HAZARDS

Some plants can be toxic for cats and may harm their skin or do them internal damage if they swallow them. To avoid unnecessary risk, it may be best to get rid of all pot plants.

MAKING YOUR HOME COMPLETELY SAFE

The domestic environment can be full of dangers for cats, such as plants and cut flowers. There are between 200 and 300 hundred plants that can harm cats if they eat them. The lily family is the most dangerous, but other plants that need to be avoided include climbing ivy, Ceylon creeper (devil's ivy), poinsettia, narcissus and hyacinth.

If you think your cat has ingested a toxin, take her to the vet at once.

1

Protect electric cables

Many cats like chewing on electric cables, running the risk of an electric shock. You should either hide your cables or protect them with special casings.

What's this?

Don't scold your cat

There's no point telling your cat off for chewing electric cables. She won't understand the reason and will only remember the unpleasant experience of being reprimanded.

I want some too!

2

Always clear the table

Human food can be harmful for a cat (see page 157), as can medicines and food supplements; never leave them lying around.

3

Keep things tidy

If your cat likes breaking or knocking over your favourite possessions, remember this is just normal cat behaviour. It's up to you to keep things you value out of reach to stop them ending up in pieces.

Tidying up?

Hide things of value

Things made of leather, such as shoes, can receive unwelcome attention from your cat's claws. It's best to put them away in a cupboard.

THE RIGHT WAY TO USE A PET CAGE

A large pet cage can be used for a short time if you have a boisterous kitten who's in danger of getting stuck between pieces of furniture.

GET A NICE TALL CAGE

If your kitten is especially adventurous and at risk of getting into a scrape while you are out, you could put her in a specially designed cage. The bigger the cage, the better. As cats like to climb, the height of the cage matters more than the floor-space. It's best if the bars are made of steel or plastic so that the kitten's claws don't get caught in them.

If you have several cats who get on well, you can leave them in the same cage. If they don't get on, you'll need a separate one for each.

My very own apartment!

1

How to furnish a cage

You absolutely must put your cat's litter tray in her cage, along with her food and water bowls. As cats don't like their toilet area to be too near where they eat, you should put the litter tray at ground level and the bowls slightly separate (ideally higher up).

What you shouldn't put in a cage
It's not a good idea to put extra heating inside a pet cage. If your cat sleeps close to it for hours, she could end up with burns.

ZZZ

2

Where to put the cage

Don't put the cage somewhere that's in full sun or complete darkness. Even at night, there should be a small amount of light in your cat's environment. Your living room is generally a good choice.

Cages and kittens
When you need to go out and leave your kitten home alone, it's sensible to put her in her cage, as the house is full of things that could attract her curiosity and expose her to danger.

3

Toys for the cage

Put toys in the cage so that your cat doesn't get bored, but avoid small toys that your cat could swallow. Larger balls or reasonably thick ropes are a good choice.

Avoid small objects
Don't leave small balls, string or ribbons in her cage. If your cat swallows them, she may suffer from an intestinal blockage.

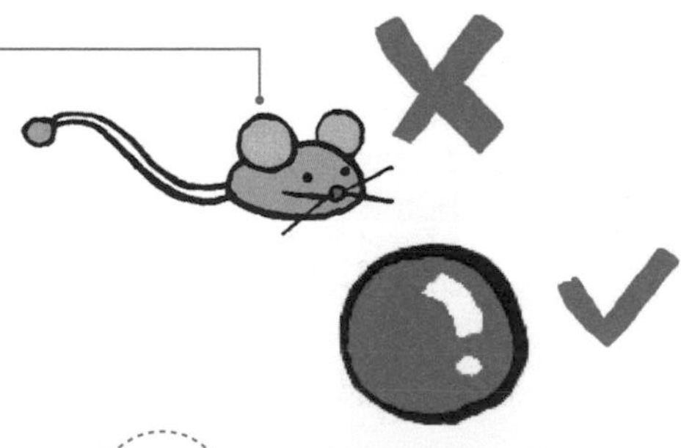

A CAT TREE MAKES LIFE FUN

Cats love to perch in high places. A cat tree can be both a place to play and a place to sleep.

AN INVITATION TO EXERCISE

Cats' wild ancestors lived in trees so they could spot their prey more easily and protect themselves from predators. Their domesticated relatives have retained that love of heights.

To satisfy their desire and encourage them to take exercise, it's a very good idea to provide cats with places they can climb and have fun. The easiest solution is to buy a cat tree or set up a climbing maze using wall-mounted cat shelves.

1

The ideal place for a cat tree

If you put the cat tree near a window, your cat will feel like she's in her very own watch tower.

Nothing to report!

Cats love looking out
To stop your cat getting bored, give her a place to watch what's going on outside.

I feel good...

Alternatives to a cat tree
If you can't provide a cat tree, try to arrange storage boxes or chairs so that your cat can use them to climb to the top of a cupboard or bookcase.

2

The high life

You'll find there is a large choice of cat trees on offer – some even include baskets and "igloos".

3

Home-made cat trees

If you're keen to try making your own cat tree, ensure it's robust enough to withstand your cat jumping and playing on it.

Is it safe?

Harder than it looks
If you're unsure about your skill level, don't shy away from calling in a professional.

COSY BEDDING TO SLEEP IN

Cats don't only sleep in their beds. They can make themselves comfortable on the back of a sofa, in a linen basket or even on a household appliance.

LET THEM CHOOSE

Cats spend a lot of their time asleep, so a comfy bed is important. Every cat has her own preferences, which can vary according to her age and the time of year. If your cat turns up her nose at the luxury basket you've bought her, don't be cross: she simply wants to choose her own bed. If you have several cats, they need at least one bed each.

1

The best place for her bed

It goes without saying that a cat's bed needs to be somewhere calm. But you should be able to see it, so that you can make sure she's OK.

The perfect bed
If you give your cat a bed that's just right for her size, there is a high chance of it being a hit. If her bed's too big, it'll be harder for her to maintain her body temperature.

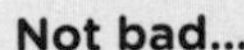

2

The right temperature

Your cat needs to have the freedom to move between warm and cool spots, so she can regulate her temperature.

How they choose
Cats always choose a sleeping place that makes them feel calm and safe, and has comfortable levels of heat and humidity.

3

Non-edible bedding

It's a good idea to line your cat's bed with a favourite blanket. Don't put fleece or wool in the bed if she's likely to chew it though.

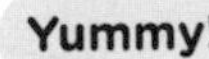

Winter warmer
To stop your cat getting cold, give her a hot water bottle in winter.

CHOOSING CAT LITTER

Some owners use so-called "self-cleaning" cat litter trays, which are supposedly more convenient and less smelly. But it's far from certain that cats actually like them.

LITTER TRAYS SHOULD NEVER SMELL

The perfect litter tray should be at least one-and-a-half times the length of your cat. Even bigger is better. It should also be sufficiently deep to prevent too much litter spilling over the edge when your cat covers her poo. Fill the tray to at least 3cm deep with litter.

It's also advisable to use an open tray (without a lid), to stop smells building up.

1

How many litter trays?

While you're asleep or out of the house, no one's cleaning the litter tray, so the ideal is to have one tray per cat, plus one extra.

Older cats
Make a little ramp to help older cats get to their litter tray and ease the strain on achy joints (see page 138 for more on this).

A brand-new tray
Initially, fill a new tray with used litter, which will smell familiar to your cat. This will make her much more likely to take to it.

2

The ideal litter

There are lots of different types of litter on the market. Go for a mineral litter with a texture close to sand.

Try out different types
You'll get to know which litter your cat prefers if you try her out on different brands.

3

Where to put the litter tray

Allow your cat to go to the toilet in peace: don't put her litter tray in a passage or a noisy place.

Not in complete darkness
If you put her litter tray somewhere that is completely dark after you turn the lights out, your cat won't be able to find her way.

THE PERFECT SCRATCHING POST

You can buy scratching posts in many different shapes and materials. There are even baskets with scratching material on the sides.

I need to do
this every day!

IT'S PART OF BEING A CAT

Your cat has an irresistible urge to scratch; pages 60–61 give more details on this innate behaviour. But it's never pleasant discovering your favourite furniture and wallpaper have been shredded.

For domestic harmony, it's vital to provide your cat with a scratching post. It's a good idea to place it near furniture and anything made of leather that would otherwise bear the brunt of her scratching.

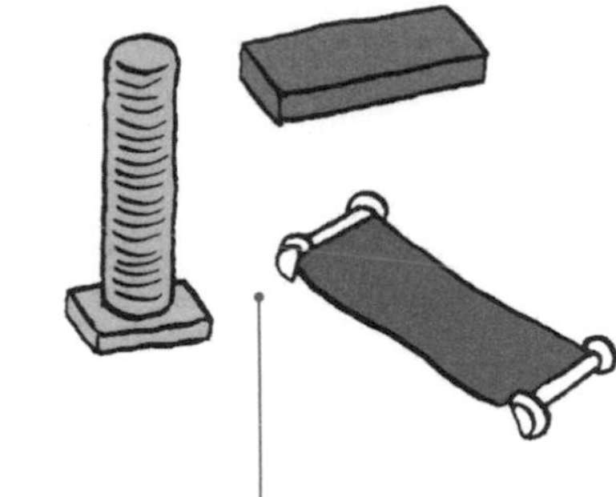

1

Try out different posts

Scratching posts can be made from many different materials: wood, cardboard, jute, carpet, etc. Every cat has her own preferences, so let her pick a favourite after she's tried a few out.

Which material?
Jute is good at catching the claws and doesn't make much mess. Cardboard is cheap but tends to be messier. Wood is closest to what cats use in the wild. A carpet-covered scratching post is resilient but costly.

My lovely sharp claws...

2

How many scratching posts?

If you have enough room, get a few different scratching posts. You can put them flat on the ground or vertically against a wall.

Where to put them
Place them near furniture and possessions that you want to protect from your pet's claws. If you rub a new post with catnip or spritz on some pheromone spray, your cat's unlikely to be able to resist.

3

Training a kitten to use a scratching post

Place your kitten in front of a scratching post, then take her two front legs and move them to imitate a scratching motion. Your kitten will leave her scent on the post, which will encourage her to use it again.

Replace them regularly
A scratching post enables your cat to replace old claws with new growth. Over time, an old post will no longer be effective for sharpening her claws.

?
Like this?

A SAFE HOME FOR AN OLDER CAT

Make sure you adapt your cat's living space as she grows older and her physical abilities decline.

CREATING A SAFE ENVIRONMENT

A young cat needs to be active to strengthen her bones and muscles. That's why she requires a cat tree to climb on.

As she ages, she will lose her physical strength, so to avoid her getting injured in a fall, it's a good idea to remove her tree when you see the first signs of ageing, around the age of thirteen or fourteen. A cat can break a bone in a fall, even from the back of a sofa.

1

Deteriorating

As she ages, your cat may have trouble perceiving her environment. Don't move your furniture around unless you have to, as this could disorientate her.

Tell-tale signs
If your cat no longer looks at you, she may have lost her sight. If her miaow is getting louder, she's likely to be hard of hearing.

2

Mind the thermostat

Older cats have trouble regulating their body temperature. Try to minimize the temperature difference between the window and the centre of the room, and between inside the home and out.

Cats and humidity
Air that is too dry is bad for cats. You can use a humidifier to raise the humidity in your home to 50% if need be.

3

Minimize the risk of accidents

To reduce the chances of your elderly cat taking a tumble, remove her tree and fit a stair gate.

Still game
Older cats tend to become sedentary as it's harder for them to climb. To encourage your cat to move, keep engaging in play with her – just stay at floor level.

MOVING HOUSE WITHOUT STRESSING YOUR CAT

When you move house, try not to buy lots of new things. If you take much of your old furniture and your cat's familiar things (litter tray, bowls) with you, your new home will smell more reassuring to your cat.

Something looks different...

LESSEN THE IMPACT

A house move is always a major upset to a cat's daily routine. Leaving somewhere familiar for a new home can be stressful for us and our pets. Meticulous planning is the key to keeping stress levels to a minimum.

1

Risk of a runaway

On the day you move, the door of the house will be open a lot of the time. And removal men coming and going can scare your cat. You should consider putting her in her pet carrier to make sure she doesn't run off.

Send her on holiday
Comings and goings can cause your cat stress, so why not have her looked after while you get on with moving?

2

Health problems after the move

It varies from cat to cat, but some animals adapt to their new home in days, whereas others take weeks. Some lose their appetite after a move. If symptoms persist, take her to the vet.

Appetite loss
It's important to have concrete information for the vet, such as the quantity of food she eats each day and how often she uses her litter tray.

3

Find a new vet

Your cat may fall ill because of the stress of moving house, so it's a good idea to identify a vet near your new home even before you move.

Choose a vet nearby
Always choose a vet who's less than half an hour from where you live.

A PET CARRIER FOR TRIPS OUT

You can't take cats out on a lead, as they aren't suited to it. You'll need a pet carrier to transport your cat.

A PLASTIC PET CARRIER THAT OPENS ON TOP

You can find many different types of carrier but for trips to the vet, I recommend the sort that opens on top. Your vet may even be able to examine your cat without taking her out of the carrier. Plastic pet carriers are easiest to clean and your cat's claws won't catch on them.

1

Getting used to a pet carrier

If you only get the pet carrier out for visits to the vet, your cat will become wary every time she sees it. But if she gets used to seeing it around the home, she'll be comfortable getting in and out of it.

How big?
It's a good idea to choose a pet carrier big enough for your cat to stretch out her legs when she's lying down. Remember to line the base with a towel or blanket.

2

Travelling with your cat

If you're travelling in a car, put your cat in her pet carrier and position it securely in the foot well in front of an empty seat. If you have to leave your cat in the car on a hot day, open the window a crack.

On public transport
Always keep your cat in her pet carrier. Avoid travelling at rush hour as she'll find that very stressful.

3

At the vet's

Don't take your cat of out the pet carrier in the waiting room. The presence of other animals may scare her. If she gets especially stressed out, you could cover her carrier with a towel.

On a long trip
Line her carrier with absorbent towels. On long car journeys, try to take your cat out of the carrier every so often to let her stretch her legs.

While you wait
The vet's waiting room is a good place to meet other cat owners and possibly pick up useful cat care tips. Just make sure your cat is feeling secure if you get chatting!

EXTRA NOTES

5

THE IDEAL ROOM FOR A CAT

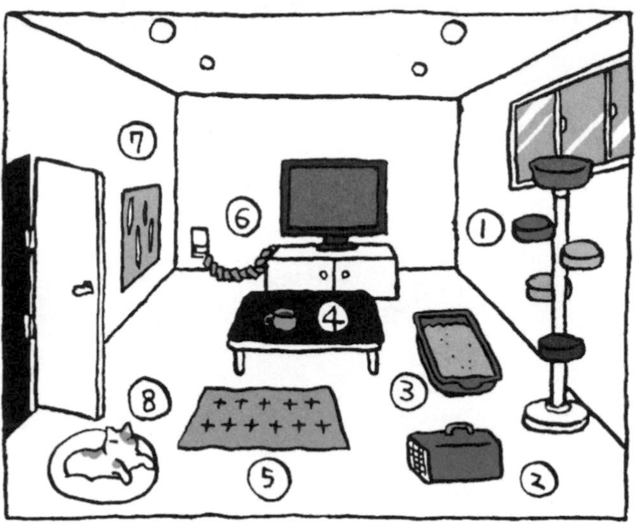

① Cat tree
Cats like being high up and a cat tree lets them practise their climbing skills. When they reach the age of thirteen or fourteen, remove the tree and encourage them to play on the floor.

② Pet carrier
To get your cat used to her pet carrier, leave it accessible so that she becomes familiar with it. The best carriers are plastic and open on top.

③ Litter tray
The perfect litter tray is large and deep and has no cover. You should put it in a quiet place near where she spends most of her time.

④ Table tops
Don't leave food or medicines lying around. And keep fragile and precious things out of your cat's way.

⑤ Fresh air
Some cats don't like air-conditioning. In summer, give her a cooling mat or leave doors open so that she settles at the ideal temperature.

⑥ Electrical cables
Many cats enjoy chewing electric cables, so hide them out of the way or fit protective covers.

⑦ Scratching post
Sharpening their claws by scratching is innate behaviour for cats. To stop her shredding your furniture and wallpaper, give her a scratching post.

⑧ Bed
Give her several comfy places to choose from, but make sure she's not completely out of sight. Your cat will pick where she wants to sleep depending on her mood.

CHAPTER

6

A LONG AND HAPPY LIFE

IT'S A CAT'S LIFE

Various factors determine a cat's life expectancy, and they don't age at the same pace as we do.

LIFE EXPECTANCY

Lifestyle affects a cat's life expectancy. On average, cats who are kept indoors live to around fifteen; for those who are allowed out, it's twelve, and for a feral cat, from five to ten. For indoor cats, life expectancy has increased markedly in recent years because of medical advances and more health-conscious owners. The habit of feeding cats on our scraps has all but died out in favour of specially produced cat food, which also helps.

The phases of a cat's life

Phase of life	Age of cat	Human equivalent	Specific needs
Kitten This is the time in a cat's life when they are most boisterous and also when they learn basic social skills.	0–1 month	0–1 years	Make sure your cat doesn't swallow things they shouldn't and take them to the vet for check-ups, neutering and vaccinations.
	2–3 months	2–4 years	
	4 months	5–8 years	
	6 months	10 years	
Junior In this period, a cat reaches sexual maturity: between five and twelve months for females and between eight and twelve months for males.	7 months	12 years	From the age of six months, cats can be neutered as long as they weigh over 2.5kg. This is the time to switch to food formulated for adult cats.
	12 months	15 years	
	18 months	21 years	
	2 years	24 years	
Prime Cats in this phase are full of energy and in peak physical condition. Feral cats in this age range may project a "leader of the pack" confidence.	3 years	28 years	During this period, cats are in their finest physical and mental health, but that doesn't mean you should miss their annual check-up at the vet's.
	4 years	32 years	
	5 years	36 years	
	6 years	40 years	
Mature A cat's physical abilities will start to decline from here. Before recent medical advances, cats were classed as "senior" by this age.	7 years	44 years	
	8 years	48 years	
	9 years	52 years	
	10 years	56 years	
Senior Around the age of thirteen, the first signs of ageing begin to affect the eyes, leg joints and claws.	11 years	60 years	Cats at this life stage start to lose agility and health problems begin to appear.
	12 years	64 years	
	13 years	68 years	
	14 years	72 years	
Geriatric By now a cat will be increasingly sedentary. It's best to try to avoid any disruption to their environment and leave them in peace as much as possible.	15 years	76 years	With their senses declining, cats in this phase of their lives find change much harder to cope with. If you can, try to avoid moving house or even changing your furniture around.
	16 years	80 years	
	17 years	84 years	
	18 years	88 years	
	19 years	92 years	
	20 years	96 years	
	21 years	100 years	
	22 years	104 years	
	23 years	108 years	
	24 years	112 years	
	25 years	116 years	

Based on information from the AAFP (American Association of Feline Practitioners) and the AAHA (American Animal Hospital Association).

CHOOSING A VET

There are an increasing number of veterinary clinics which specialize in feline medicine. Choose the one best suited to your cat.

YOUR CAT'S WELLBEING AS TOP PRIORITY

Many cats are stressed by a visit to the vet. One solution is to choose somewhere that specializes in cats only.

Another solution is to rely on the International Society of Feline Medicine's "Cat Friendly Clinic" programme, which compiles a register of veterinary practices that pay particular attention to the welfare of cats.*

To feature on the register, clinics need to meet over 100 criteria, such as having separate waiting areas for dogs and cats, and cat-only consulting rooms.

**The International Society of Feline Medicine (ISFM) is a worldwide resource for cat medicine and surgery.*

Very important!

How to choose a good vet

Go through all these questions before you decide on a vet for your cat:

- [ ] Are the waiting area and consultation rooms clean?
- [ ] Does the vet provide enough detail on the illness, treatment and any test required?
- [ ] Is my cat handled with care?
- [ ] Does the vet demonstrate sufficient expertise?
- [ ] Does the vet give information about the cost of tests and treatment up-front?
- [ ] Is the bill detailed and easy to understand?
- [ ] Does the vet answer all my questions?
- [ ] Is the practice nearby, and will the vet do home visits if necessary?
- [ ] Is the vet happy to seek a second opinion from colleagues?
- [ ] Do I get on well with the vet?

ADDING UP THE COST

You can't skimp on the cost of keeping your cat in good health. Ultimately, treating an illness will always cost more than spending money on your cat's wellbeing throughout her life.

PUT MONEY ASIDE FOR A RAINY DAY

Bringing a cat into your life costs money. She may live for eighteen years, during which time she'll need regular check-ups and booster vaccinations from the vet. And after the age of ten, her more delicate health will mean that medical bills could stack up. You should always be prepared to spend what's needed for her welfare: high-quality food and visits to the vet, for example.

1

Most British cat owners spend around £500 a year on food, plus basic vet bills of around £200 for things like a health check, vaccination, parasite control and dental hygiene. The annual cost will depend on the age of the cat, but you might well spend £15,000 over the cat's lifetime.

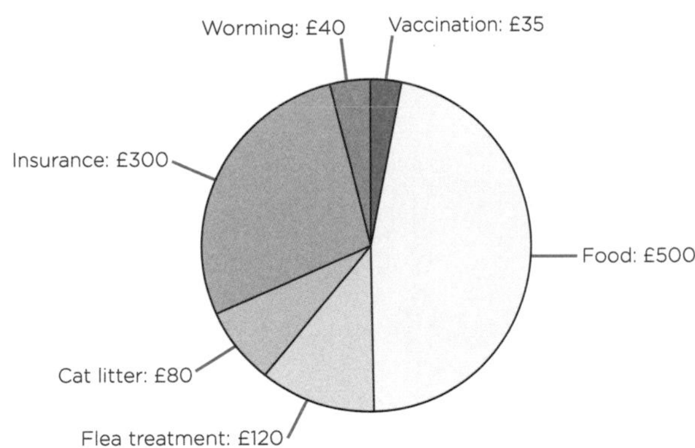

Note: this information is for guidance only. Expenditure varies according to the cat (breed, age, underlying health) and kittens are more expensive in their first year.

2

Initial costs (when your cat first comes to your home)

Bowls: £10	Pet carrier: £40
Scratching post: £30	Safety collar: £5
Litter tray: £30	Toys: £20
Bed: £25	Grooming brush: £15

3

Pet insurance is a must

It's a very good idea to get pet insurance for your cat right from the start, as it will get more expensive as she grows older. Try to set aside some money in advance of health problems or other unexpected events.

BREED-SPECIFIC AILMENTS

So-called pedigree cats are a human creation. Before you decide to acquire one, it's important to know their characteristics.

A PREDISPOSITION TO PARTICULAR HEALTH PROBLEMS

Pedigree cats are the product of selective breeding over multiple generations in order to meet certain breed standards. This can produce individuals who come from a genetically reduced stock – even the progeny of blood relatives – with a predisposition to certain hereditary conditions. This is why it's important to know both the illnesses and character traits specific to each breed.

Pedigree cat diseases

The following is a select list of breeds and the diseases they are prone to. In addition to this list, it's also worth noting that the Norwegian forest cat can suffer from glycogenosis (metabolic disorder caused by enzyme deficiency) and hypertrophic cardiomyopathy (thickening of the heart muscles), Bengals from peripheral neuropathy (nervous system damage), Siamese from epidermolysis nervosa (skin blistering) and British shorthairs from renal polycystosis (kidney cysts).

	Breed	Character	Genetically predisposed to
Large breeds (over 5 kg)	**Maine Coon**	**Affectionate, even-tempered**	Hypertrophic cardiomyopathy (thickening of the heart muscles)
	Ragdoll	**Calm, even-tempered**	Hypertrophic cardiomyopathy
Medium-sized breeds (3–5 kg)	**Scottish fold**	**Mild**	Osteochondrodysplasias (abnormal bone and cartilage development), hypertrophic cardiomyopathy
	Munchkin	**Active, playful**	Pectus excavatum (funnel chest), joint and skin problems
	American shorthair	**Even-tempered, active**	Hypertrophic cardiomyopathy
	Abyssinian	**Active, playful**	Blood, liver, eye and skin problems, renal amyloidosis (protein build-up leading to kidney failure)
	Persian	**Even-tempered**	Kidney, eye and skin diseases
Small breeds (2–3 kg)	**Singapura**	**Even-tempered, affectionate**	Pyruvate kinase deficiency (metabolic disorder)

COMMON DISEASES

If your cat develops a disease, it's important to identify the first symptoms quickly.

The main diseases affecting cats

Key:

 Disease that can be avoided if the cat is vaccinated and doesn't go outside

 Disease that can be avoided if the cat is vaccinated

S Symptom

Disease	Symptoms and prevention	Disease	Symptoms and prevention
Feline immuno-deficiency virus (FIV or "cat AIDS")	This virus is passed on during catfights. Once a cat has the disease, she has it for life, but the condition can be asymptomatic.	Bronchitis / pneumonia	This disease develops from a simple cold, but rapidly becomes more serious and requires urgent medical attention.
	S Dysfunction of the immune system, chronic stomatitis (inflammation of the mouth).		**S** Cough, fever, breathing problems.
Feline leukaemia (FELV)	FELV is a virus transmitted through the saliva, or from mother to foetus. Once signs present, there is little prospect of cure.	Feline lymphoma	This is a form of cancer affecting the lymphocytes.
	S Loss of appetite, fever, diarrhoea, anaemia, tumours.		**S** Lack of appetite and weight loss. This form of cancer is often detected late.

Disease	Symptoms and prevention	Disease	Symptoms and prevention
Feline viral rhinotracheitis (FVR)	This virus is passed on through nasal secretion or saliva. When a cat contracts the disease, she becomes a carrier for life, though symptoms may only present later.	Mammary tumour	Tumours can affect the mammary glands of older female cats. They prove malignant in 90% of cases and can metastasize to the lungs and lymphatic ganglions.
	S Sneezing, runny nose, fever, conjunctivitis.		**S** Appearance of nodules around the breasts or stomach.
Feline panleucopenia	This is a highly contagious disease which often proves fatal. It causes intestinal inflammation and reduced white blood cell count.	Diabetes	This disease results from raised blood sugar levels. Its clinical manifestations seem less severe than in human patients.
	S Fever, vomiting, bloody stools. Kittens are especially prone to violent vomiting and diarrhoea.		**S** Excessive urination, excessive thirst, vomiting, walking on hocks, loss of weight despite no loss of appetite. Often affects cats who are obese.
Feline calicivirus	**S** This is a respiratory disease transmitted through contact with a cat who is carrying the virus.	Hyperthyroid	An excess of thyroid hormones causes an acceleration of the metabolism, and therefore increased energy expenditure. Mainly affects cats over the age of eight.
	Weepy eyes, salivation, sneezing. In the severest cases, stomatitis or ulceration of the tongue. Kittens and older cats are most at risk.		**S** Weight loss despite increased appetite, hyperactivity, aggression. Early diagnosis is desirable.
Feline chlamydiosis	**S** This disease is transmitted through contact with a cat who carries the bacterium.	Cystitis	This is an inflammation of the bladder caused by the formation of urinary stones.
	Sneezing, cough, weepy eyes, conjunctivitis. Early diagnosis is desirable.		**S** Frequent urination, with traces of blood in the urine. This condition can be prevented by getting the cat to drink enough water.
Feline infectious peritonitis (FIP)	**S** This is an inflammation of the peritoneum and the pleura. It can take the form of a pronounced inflammation of the eyes and kidneys. It's a fatal condition.	Megacolon	This is caused by a problem with the functioning of the colon, which becomes abnormally dilated, preventing the cat from excreting.
	Swollen abdomen and thorax, loss of appetite, fever, diarrhoea. Stress is an aggravating factor.		**S** Constipation, loss of appetite, vomiting. To prevent this condition, address the problem of constipation.

FOODS TO AVOID

Some foods that humans eat quite happily are toxic to cats, though their harmful effects may not appear until long after they were consumed. This means that food is often overlooked as a possible culprit when a cat falls ill.

CATS SHOULD STICK TO CAT FOOD

Many of the foods we eat can poison cats or cause long-term health problems. When your cat gazes up at you while you're eating, don't be tempted to give her something from your plate as it can quickly become a habit: your cat will keep begging for food, or even steal it, which may cause food poisoning.

Foods that are dangerous for cats

Low risk (!) Medium risk (!!) High risk (!!!)

	Dangerous foods	Risks to health
Fruit and vegetables	Onions, leeks, spring onions, chives, garlic (!!!)	The enzyme alliinase in these vegetables destroys white blood cells. Cats can reach a state of anaemia in two or three days and acute kidney failure within a week.
	Avocado (!!)	Avocados contain the toxin persin, which can cause convulsions and breathing difficulties in cats.
Fish and seafood	Mackerel, sardine, tuna (!)	Overconsumption of saturated fatty acids can cause jaundice: inflammation of the fat around organs and the appearance of nodules, fever and pains.
Meat	Raw pork (!)	Pork can be infected with the parasite that causes toxoplasmosis. While this doesn't cause acute symptoms in cats, it can be passed on to humans through contact with cat poo. Pregnant women should exercise particular caution.
	Liver in large quantities (!!)	If a cat eats too much liver, it can cause an excess of vitamin A, which may result in bone deformation.
Other foods	Spicy condiments (!!)	Cats experience the fiery effects of pepper and chilli far more severely than we do.
	Chocolate (!!!)	The theobromine contained in chocolate is toxic to cats, causing nervous and digestive problems, shaking, fever and convulsions. In the severest cases, it can prove fatal.
	Grapes and raisins (!!)	Eating grapes has recently been proven to be harmful to dogs. As their possible effects on cats are still unknown, it is best to err on the side of caution and avoid them.

A CHANGING DIET FOR EACH PHASE OF LIFE

The way you feed your cat matters just as much as what's in her bowl.

GET YOUR KITTEN USED TO A VARIETY OF FOODS

Cats' nutritional needs will change as they go through life. You should pay particular attention to the needs of kittens and older cats. Once kittens have been weaned, it's a good idea to feed them kitten food from a variety of different brands to prevent them becoming fussy eaters.

And it's also advisable to feed older cats a special senior formula, adjusting the portion size according to body type and level of activity.

Dietary advice by age group

Phase of life		Advice and precautions
Kitten (up to six months)	**Suckling** (up to four weeks)	After giving birth to her litter, a mother cat secretes a liquid called colostrum, which gives the kittens immunity from micro-organisms. If kittens are unable to suckle immediately after birth, they're likely to miss out on this immunity. It's preferable to vaccinate them as soon as possible.
	Weaning (up to two months)	The process of weaning begins around the age of four weeks, when the milk teeth begin to come through. Kittens should gradually be introduced to specially formulated kitten food over the course of one to two weeks. Because their energy requirement is three or four times greater than that of an adult cat, kitten food is high in calories and as kittens have small stomachs, their daily food intake should be divided into four or five meals.
	Growth phase (two to six months)	Kittens are highly active during this phase and need to be fed special food that is easy for them to digest but high in protein and calories. If a kitten is healthy, you can allow her to eat as much as she wants. But keep an eye on her stools; if they're too soft, reduce the quantity of food you're giving her. Neutured cats need less food.
Junior (seven months to two years)		A cat's daily food intake should be calculated according to her weight and activity level. A very active cat should eat 65 kcal of food for every kilo that she weighs, whereas an indoor cat needs only 45 kcal. Follow the guidelines on the back of your food packet and adjust portion size to take account of your cat's weight, level of activity and appetite.
Adult (three to ten years)		This tends to be a relatively stable period in a cat's life, in terms of both health and temperament. But some cats put on weight at this age, which can cause a number of diseases, so make sure you feed yours a balanced, not too calorific diet. If you do give treats, make sure they don't add up to more than 10% of your cat's daily intake.
Senior (eleven to fourteen years)		This is the time to switch to special food for senior cats and to be vigilant for changes in your cat's appetite and state of health. A senior cat is more vulnerable to disease, as her immune system and general health begin to decline. If your cat's water consumption changes, this may indicate a health problem. And loss of appetite may be a sign that she has inflammation of the gums.
Geriatric (over fifteen years)		Keep feeding your cat pellets for as long as she is able to eat solid food. But if she loses her appetite, try her on wet food or soften her dry food with water. Don't skimp on regular health check-ups. And if you have any concerns, take her to the vet.

AFTERWORD

A few years ago, I went to an international seminar on animal behaviour. One of the people there made this observation: "A dog looks at her owners and thinks, 'They give me shelter and food. They love and protect me. They must be gods!' But a cat's thought process is: 'These humans give me food and shelter. They love and protect me. That means I must be the god!'"

This does capture what might be called "cat psychology" rather well. After all, who can be sure that our cats don't regard us as their faithful servants?

While it's true that cats are usually less demonstrative than dogs, that doesn't mean they don't have emotions. To tune in to the subtle messages that cats are trying to send us, we just need a bit of basic knowledge, along with a few tricks and tips.

As a cat owner, it's important to keep asking yourself how best to understand your cat and encourage her to return your love, as well as how to keep her healthy for as long as possible.

My hope is that this book has helped you to understand your cat, and that it will contribute to your happy life together.

Dr. Yuki Hattori
Tokyo Feline Medical Center